Spirituality and Self-Esteem:
Developing the Inner Self

Spirituality and Self-Esteem: Developing the Inner Self

Richard L. Bednar
Scott R. Peterson

Deseret Book Company
Salt Lake City, Utah

All of the major concepts and ideas about self-esteem in this book were originally put forward in a volume entitled *Self-Esteem: Paradoxes and Innovations in Clinical Theory and Practice,* written by Richard L. Bednar, Gawain M. Wells, and Scott R. Peterson and published for mental-health professionals by the American Psychological Association. Materials included in the present work have been summarized, abbreviated, paraphrased, or quoted by permission of the original authors and the publisher.

Library of Congress Cataloging-in-Publication Data

Bednar, Richard L.
   Spirituality and self-esteem : developing the inner self / by
  Richard L. Bednar and Scott R. Peterson.
     p. cm.
   Includes index.
   ISBN 0-87579-360-6 (hard)
   1. Spiritual life — Mormon authors. 2. Self-respect — Religious
aspects — Mormon Church. 3. Self-realization — Religious aspects —
Mormon Church. 4. Spirituality — Mormon Church. 5. Mormon Church —
Doctrines. 6. Church of Jesus Christ of Latter-day Saints —
Doctrines. I. Peterson, Scott R. II. Title.
BX8656.B44   1990
248.4'89332 — dc20   90-40728
                                            CIP

Printed in the United States of America

10   9   8   7   6   5   4   3   2   1

Table of Contents

Preface, vii

Chapter One
Appearances: Compliance or Conviction? 1

Chapter Two
The Eternal Self, 15

Chapter Three
Spirituality: What It Is, Where It Comes From,
and What It Does, 20

Chapter Four
Self-Esteem: What It Is, Where It Comes From,
and What It Does, 32

Chapter Five
Integrating Spirituality and Self-Esteem, 49

Chapter Six
Cultivating Self-Esteem, 79

Chapter Seven
Cultivating Spirituality, 112

Chapter Eight
Spirituality and Self-Esteem: Putting It All Together, 132

Index, 153

v

Preface

The truth is usually provocative and always potent. Like a wolf exposing its underbelly, it can be soft and warm, unthreatening and pleasant. Yet, when it turns over, baring fangs both sharp and cold, it can be dangerous and unpredictable. Far too many of us have underestimated the power of truth to expose and humiliate as well as to clarify and enlighten. Nevertheless, we all praise truth's virtue. We praise its pursuit. Nothing has been so sought after, fought over, and misunderstood. It is highly valued in political and business arenas and yet is woefully absent in both. We expect it of our children, spouses, and friends. When we don't get it, we are disappointed and hurt. Yet when we do get it, we may be hurt just the same. When it comes to acknowledging our own weaknesses, shortcomings, and fears, this self-same truth is what we so naturally are inclined to deny, distort, and avoid.

How can we be so willing, often so compelled, to avert our eyes from the truth of what we are and wish not to be, a truth that we wish to hide from ourselves and others, a truth that we must recognize before it can no longer be the truth?

In a gospel context, the truth is paramount in our striving for exaltation. Truth "shall make [us] free" (John 8:32). "Truth abideth forever" (D&C 1:39). We look to "the way, the truth, and the life" for eternal guidance and direction (John 14:6).

So, although this book is about spirituality and self-esteem and how they relate to perfecting the internal self, it is also about the pursuit of truth, personal truth—the truth of what we are and what we may become. Our discussions of spirituality and self-esteem focus on the importance of acknowledging the truth about ourselves. The ability to truthfully evaluate one's behavior, motives, and feelings nurtures self-esteem and spirituality.

In both ecclesiastical and professional experiences, we have found that the condition that allows for the most growth is individuals' ability to confront what most they fear about themselves. Yet in a world that not only condones false appearances but demands and thrives on phony outward impressions, it is the exception, not the rule, for its inhabitants to be willing to recognize their own weaknesses for fear that others will as well. The result is a never-ending pursuit of glitz, glamour, and gratification, none of which is capable of bringing the happiness they all so deceptively promise. And so the paradox continues: happiness is sought by covering up the very truth which, if confronted, could bring the happiness so many desperately desire!

In Chapter 1 we talk about society's tendency to perpetuate facades. We see how spirituality and self-esteem are not impervious to this tendency, and we examine the essential elements of both these qualities. In Chapter 2 we define the internal self in relation to our eternal identities. In Chapter 3 we take an in-depth look at spirituality—what it is, as well as what it is not. In Chapter 4 we focus on a model of self-esteem developed by Dr. Bednar and his associates at Brigham Young University. This innovative model asserts that self-evaluation is essential to self-esteem: the process of being aware of, paying attention to, and then evaluating our own behavior. We suggest that self-evaluations will be positive or negative according to our tendency either to consistently cope with what we fear or to consistently avoid it, whether what we fear is a relationship, an important task at work, church, or school, or a characteristic about ourselves that keeps us from becoming the type of person we want to be. In Chapter 5 we discuss the relationship between spirituality and self-esteem and how their development follows the same process on different planes — one being spiritual, and the other, temporal. In Chapters 6 and 7 we describe the steps and the ingredients essential in cultivating spirituality and self-esteem. In Chapter 8 a case study drawn from real life shows the relationship of the internal/eternal self to spirituality and self-esteem.

Throughout the book we rely heavily on stories to illustrate the principles we introduce. We hope they entertain as well as inform. We hope, further, that this book allows you to find the truth about yourself, so that the truth will indeed make you free.

Chapter One

Appearances: Compliance or Conviction?

Out of bed in the morning. Clean up. Look in the full-length mirror. Then in a deep and deliberate voice, repeat your fifty self-affirmations: "I am a good person, I am a confident person, I am a good person, I am a confident person," and so on. You attempt to persuade yourself that you are something better than you believe you really are. This technique is usually called positive self-talk, or something similar. What you call it doesn't really matter. It's a way of trying to feel better, of being more positive in your outlook, and of recognizing your strengths. But can words really do that? Does thinking it, and then saying it, really make it so? It's not like dieting to lose weight or exercising to build muscles. Do words really change things?

That approach to facing difficult problems is a prescription contained in many reputable self-help books. It is founded on one basic assumption: How you think determines how you feel, and what you think is revealed by what you say. If you have a problem with low self-esteem, it's because you have negative self-thoughts. So, the formula asks, do you want to improve your self-image? Then get out of bed in the morning, clean up, stand in front of a full-length mirror, and in a deep and deliberate voice, repeat your fifty self-affirmations: "I am a good person, I am a confident person." And if it looks like it's going to be a tough day, you may want to go through an extra fifteen or twenty.

Can saying it make it happen? Can verbal pretense make it real? It's an interesting thought, and one that has much to recommend it. It's quick, cheap, and easy (maybe that should be enough to make us suspicious). But will it work? That is the real question. Will it create an enduring sense of personal peace and well-being? There is only one way to tell for sure. Go over to the mirror, and in a deep and deliberate voice start saying, "I am a good person, I am a confident person."

Well, how many people do you think actually went to the mirror and tried it? Not many, you say? But why? Because everybody knows intuitively that "saying it" doesn't automatically make it so. Words can eloquently *describe* reality, but they are not nearly so effective at *creating* it.

We must ask ourselves, then, why are we so willing to accept simple appearances in place of the real thing? This all too human tendency is as global as it is individual. And the evidence of our short-sighted foolishness is everywhere. Nations are trying to prevent nuclear war while stockpiling the very weapons they say they eschew. The protective ozone layer of our atmosphere and the rain forests of South America have become victims of our highly prized technology and much coveted profits even as we preach environmentalism. Deadly drugs have become the counterfeit substitute for a meaningful life. The foolishness of our own contradictory, self-defeating behavior is both widespread and undeniable.

In our own country we have fared little better. We tend to be more concerned with power and prosperity than with poverty and principle. And more often than not, immediacy and expediency prevail in situations where patience and perseverance are called for. We are suckers for quick profits, cosmetic solutions, and a good time. Why?

Why are we so easily satisfied by immediate gratification, superficial results, and false appearances? Most of us like things the quick and easy way. You know, a pill for pain and cash for class. We live in a world where appearances seem more important than reality, and the difference between appearance and reality is not as clear as it once was. A very successful manufacturer has made a fortune on an advertising campaign for hair coloring, which goes something like this:

A gorgeous blonde with long silky hair is lounging on a white sofa in an opulent living room. In a slow, deep voice she says, "Some people think I'm spoiled!"

There's a long pause, then the camera zooms in for a close-up of her face and hair. "Maybe I am. I use only the best, you know. That's why I use this product. It may cost a little more, but I'm worth it."

The message is clear. If you use the best, you become the best. It's that easy. A quality hair rinse makes you a quality person! We have been exposed to the Madison Avenue mentality for so long now that some of us may actually believe that the sun always shines in Florida, a deep tan is essential for personal happiness, and the style of our clothing reflects the quality of our character. That's what happens when we believe that shallow appearances can meet deeper needs. We like them, we want them, and so we buy them, hoping that our dreams will all come true, when in reality the prospect of such easy purchases becoming happiness is next to nil. We really are suckers for pleasant illusions.

There are probably few of us who have not been fooled and cheated by appearances. That is particularly true of our impressions of others, as well as others' impressions of us. Regrettably but undeniably we live in a world of interpersonal make-believe. Politicians continually insist that they are our advocates, yet they keep getting prosecuted for self-serving fraud. Many of our friends and neighbors appear to be stable, hard-working, and happy, yet in the privacy of their homes they live in conflict, tension, and discontent. In most of our social circles and Christmas-card messages, the predominant theme is family successes, accomplishments, and optimism, even though we may be on the verge of divorce, bankruptcy, and poor health. No one wants to own up to a problem, and almost everyone seems ready to accept a quick fix.

The illusion of prosperity and tranquility is selling well these days. But lurking just beneath its thin veneer are the grinding realities of daily life with its difficult choices, crying children, emotional misunderstandings, and our eager search for personal happiness that is far more elusive than most of us had imagined. Ironically, the very substance of our daily struggles eventually exposes the cheerful but bankrupt illusions to be the hollow frauds they are. Only in our struggles do the benefits of psychological and spiritual well-being come into clear and vivid focus. They will never be found in the emptiness of gilded store fronts and glossed-over season's greetings.

Are we as foolish as we look? Probably so. You see, far too many of us search in the wrong places for what we value the most. We can only wonder why creating worldly appearances and maintaining false impressions receive so much attention when the happiness we seek is to be found only *inside ourselves* as a result of our own spirituality and self-esteem.

Fundamentals of Successful Living: Spirituality and Self-Esteem

How many times have you been part of a discussion where the questions were asked: "What does it take to be happy in life?" or "What are the ingredients for successful living?" Invariably, you've probably heard people respond using such phrases as "sense of security," "meaningful relationships," "sense of accomplishment," "feelings of self-worth," "relationship with our Heavenly Father," "an understanding of who we are," and so on. Listing them is easy. Understanding and prioritizing them is more difficult. With so many different and desirable ingredients available, we must ask, What are their properties? What proportion of each should we mix and stir together in our recipe for successful living?

Tough questions, you say? We agree. But difficult or not, they must be answered, either by default or deliberation. And in our view, the two most essential elements are authentic spirituality and enduring personal self-esteem — both concepts that are frequently misunderstood and seldom considered to be as attainable as they really are. The cost of such confusion can be high, particularly in a world where the tendency to accept easier alternatives and false substitutions can and does deter us from pursuing a direction that requires greater effort but that promises greater satisfaction. We won't be offering you recipe cards, how-to lists, or quick and easy ways of "getting" spirituality and self-esteem. As you will see, spirituality and self-esteem are not things you "get." They are not acquired like an educational degree or a certificate of merit. Genuine spirituality and self-esteem are rooted in life-long processes that require constant attention and nurturing. Our purpose is to discuss these concepts and their applications to daily living with the simplicity, precision, and care they deserve. To begin to do so, we must first ask what authentic spirituality and self-esteem are, and what role they play in perfecting the internal self.

Spirituality

The first crucial characteristic of authentic spirituality is that it is essentially an *internal quality.* Obviously, this internal quality regularly influences and motivates outward behavior.

But few seem to fully understand that complying with the outward manifestations of spirituality without feeling its internal presence is nothing more than an empty imitation. And, as will be seen shortly, the scriptures are clear on this point. In authentic spirituality, outward behavior is a congruent expression of a healthy internal motive. It is as though persons actually sense the need and value of committing themselves to purposes that transcend their immediate pleasures and personal satisfaction. The motives for spiritual growth are healthy, internal, and reliable. They have little to do with fear, guilt, appearance, or compliance. They are personal, internal, and a reflection of the inner person. They spring from our eternal nature that longs for spiritual fulfillment. These motives tend to be quiet, congruent, strong, and durable when they are carefully cared for. And because of their healthy internal origins, they have more sustaining power when their durability is taxed by the burdens of righteous living. Authentic motives for spiritual growth are as essential to authentic spiritual growth as nutrition is to physical growth.

But what about desirable behavior that is not an expression of healthy internal spiritual motives and intent? There are many such motives, you know, particularly in church-related activities. It is not uncommon for people to attend church for social reasons or to study the scriptures out of a sense of duty, and, in some cases, guilt or fear. People are often gracious to others out of a need to be accepted rather than out of a genuine desire to be kind. How are we to interpret the meaning and value of behavior when such motives prevail? And why are motives so important if they can all lead to the same desirable behavior anyhow? After all, isn't high-quality Christian behavior the real test of spiritual development?

These are all important questions about which the scriptures provide clear and consistent answers. The point is almost always the same: appearances just don't count for much in spiritual domains. External compliance to rules, convention, or custom is not a substitute for internal spiritual strength and sensitivity. And outward behavior that is not an expression of internal development is generally a form of pretending that has few, if any, enduring spiritual benefits. Let us explain and illustrate.

We are all accustomed to being judged by our behavior and performance in our highly competitive western culture. It is quite natural, therefore, to assume that behavior and performance are accurate indicators of spiritual and psychological development and status. And, in some cases, they truly are. But the scriptures emphasize quite another message. Here, the value of the behavior is determined by motive and intent, not by performance and appearance. In other words, the underlying motive for the behavior reveals its authentic meaning and value.

That is hardly a trivial point in the scriptures. Paul's sermon on charity may be the most incisive and dramatic illustration of this fundamental point: "And though I bestow all my goods to feed the poor, and though I give my body to be burned, and have not charity, it profiteth me nothing" (1 Corinthians 13:3).

We find essentially the same point being made by Nephi and by Moroni:

"Verily, verily, I say that I would that ye should do alms unto the poor; but take heed that ye do not your alms before men to be seen of them; otherwise ye have no reward of your Father who is in heaven. Therefore, when ye shall do your alms do not sound a trumpet before you, as will hypocrites do in the synagogues and in the streets, that they may have glory of men. Verily I say unto you, they have their reward" (3 Nephi 13:1–2).

"For behold, God hath said a man being evil cannot do that which is good; for if he offereth a gift, or prayeth unto

7

God, except he shall do it with real intent it profiteth him nothing. For behold, it is not counted unto him for righteousness. For behold, if a man being evil giveth a gift, he doeth it grudgingly; wherefore it is counted unto him the same as if he had retained the gift; wherefore he is counted evil before God" (Moroni 7:6–8).

A latter-day prophet declared: "Mere compliance with the word of the Lord, without a corresponding inward desire, will avail but little. Indeed, such outward actions and pretending phrases may disclose hypocrisy, a sin that Jesus most vehemently condemned" (David O. McKay, *Gospel Ideals* [Salt Lake City: Deseret Book Co., 1976], p. 382).

When properly understood, these are sobering and difficult spiritual qualities to master. They leave little doubt about the primacy of motives and intent in understanding righteous behavior and spiritual development. They require a high level of internal spiritual development to be effective.

Further, these provocative and perplexing requirements introduce the possibility that church activity, no matter how successful or productive, might well be considered spiritual hypocrisy when the behavior is not a sincere and congruent expression of internal spiritual motives. These requirements can be confusing and difficult for those who have been meticulously conditioned to recognize spirituality by appearances and performance. But difficult or not, the message is clear. Spiritual growth comes from spiritual sources. The only real solution to questionable personal motives is a broken heart and a contrite spirit, which invite an awakening of our internal capacity for spirituality.

Simply shifting the emphasis from outward behavior to internal motives has monumental implications. Such a shift increases individual responsibility and accountability because no one can understand more about your private motives than you—except, of course, God. You are the one who must learn to act congruently. You are the one who must learn how to alter and improve your motives when you find them to be less than pleasing and acceptable. Overcoming selfishness is no longer a matter of giving more; it is actually wanting to give more. And you are the one who must resolve conflicts between what you are and what you hope to become. This increased personal responsibility and accountability for self-direction creates the possibility of perfecting the internal self, both spiritually and psychologically. This is not the comfortable road that passive people follow or prefer. This is the dynamic road of the spiritually minded who constantly stretch to cultivate and refine the spiritual essence of their internal identity.

Self-Esteem

The importance of self-esteem to emotional well-being is undeniable. Self-esteem is as essential to psychological well-being as the spirit is to spiritual well-being. The degree to which we find a sense of psychological contentment and happiness is largely determined by our level of self-esteem. This point of view has been suggested by prominent Church leaders as well as by psychological research. President Harold B. Lee said: "As I have prayerfully thought of the reasons why one chooses this course which is dramatically described by the prophet Isaiah—when one who has departed from the path which would have given him peace is like the troubled sea, casting up mire and dirt—it seems to me that it all results from the failure of the individual to have self-respect" (in Conference Report, Oct. 1973, p. 4).

Similarly, psychological research has consistently suggested that individuals with low self-esteem are more depressed, more accepting of external influences, and more anxious, and that they possess more characteristics that inhibit creativity, performance, effective interpersonal communications, and conflict resolution than do individuals who have high self-esteem. Low self-esteem is also consistently related to emotional problems, lack of confidence, low initiative, and low expectations for success. There are simply no favorable consequences associated with low self-esteem.

High self-esteem, on the other hand, is related to everything that seems to make us a better person. Individuals with high self-esteem tend to be better adjusted, happier, more successful, more confident, better problem-solvers, and better communicators. The list of benefits goes on and on, but the primary point is obvious. Self-esteem is a highly valued trait that directly and undeniably influences the quality of our lives.

And what exactly is self-esteem? For now, we wish to point out only that self-esteem is an internal sense of well-being. It is quiet, confident, and strong. It is a realistic appreciation of ourselves that is experienced more as a feeling or emotion than as a thought or belief. It is a form of personal internal security that allows us to function more fully, freely, and effectively in almost every facet of our lives. And the benefits of high self-esteem tend to be consistent, regardless of social class, level of achievement, or religious affiliation.

But where does this elusive trait come from? And how can it be cultivated and nourished? Those are controversial topics in psychology. The model of self-esteem we discuss represents a radical departure from the views of most contemporary psychologists. Unlike many psychological theories, it is compatible with the most fundamental tenets of Christian belief generally and of Mormon doctrine specifically. This model of self-esteem was developed by Dr. Richard Bednar and his colleagues at the Comprehensive Clinic at Brigham Young University after twenty years of clinical research and practice. It was published recently by the American Psychological Association in a new academic text entitled *Self-Esteem: Paradoxes and Innovations in Clinical Theory and Practice.*

Unlike most theorists, who assert that the approval of

others is one of the prime ingredients of self-esteem, Dr. Bednar and his colleagues suggest that the self-esteem of adults does not depend on the approval or praise of others. Rather, as adults we regularly notice what we do, how we feel, and how we feel about what we do. Our own feelings about our behavior are the substance from which our self-esteem either grows or withers. High self-esteem and low self-esteem are not the result of how others see us. Rather, they are a result of how we see ourselves. The quality of character we see in ourselves, particularly when we are confronted with problems we would prefer to avoid, determines our level of self-esteem.

Like spirituality, self-esteem is by nature internal. Although certain behaviors are often attributed to high self-esteem, self-esteem cannot be measured by outward appearances. Therein lies the critical trap. We all too readily assume that external behaviors, possessions, or praise will either produce or reflect high self-esteem, something that only the internal process of self-approval can produce, measure, and acknowledge.

The Internal Self

Even though it may not appear obvious, we each have an internal self that is often distinctly different from our public self. This internal self does not have any known physical attributes, but its influence on our lives can be substantial, both spiritually and psychologically.

The internal self is composed of two primary ingredients. The first is psychological and is called our self-concept. Our self-concept is made up of our enduring attitudes and thoughts about ourselves. It is, literally, what we perceive ourselves to be. Its content can range from confident to awkward, from capable to clumsy. It embraces all facets of our make-up and can be quite complex. If you can get your spouse or your children to start talking openly and candidly about how they really see themselves, they are telling you about their self-concept. Such a conversation would probably cover such topics as talents, limitations, fears, values, attitudes, and expectations. Self-esteem, or the regard we have for ourselves, is simply one important dimension of our self-concept. The accuracy with which we perceive ourselves is usually considered to be a good indicator of psychological adjustment. Generally speaking, the more fully and accurately we perceive the full range of events that compose our self-concept, the better adjusted we are.

From a Latter-day Saint point of view, however, there is more to the internal self than just psychological attributes and perceptions. We also have an eternal spiritual identity. Our eternal identity is everlasting and consists of an element that was never created (intelligence), combined with a part that was spiritually created by our Father in Heaven. It is important to remember that our eternal identity is unique and separate from any other in the universe, that it is essentially spiritual in nature, and that this identity existed before we were born and accompanied us into mortality. It probably has strong leanings and dispositions to favor light and truth, seek spiritual companionship, and avoid evil — at least for most of us.

Obviously, we consider spirituality and self-esteem to be the most essential dimensions of our internal well-being. They both require constant care and attention. We are, after all, living both a spiritual and a secular life. It is essential, therefore, that we be able to understand and develop ourselves in both secular and spiritual terms.

Spirituality and self-esteem share many common qualities. Both enhance our eternal capacity to love others as well as ourselves, which is one of the highest levels of human functioning. Both contribute to our internal sense of personal well-being and the eventual fulfillment of our innate potential. And perhaps most important, both are essential for us to be self-directing and self-governing.

In this book we explore both the myths and the realities of authentic and enduring spirituality and self-esteem. In the process we raise intriguing questions for your consideration. Your answers to those questions can make important differences in how you choose to live your life. Therefore, we try to discuss the relationship between spirituality and self-esteem with considerable care and precision. We also explore the concept of internal/eternal identity as it plays a major role in developing both spirituality and self-esteem. In discussing these topics, we probably challenge a number of private beliefs about self-esteem and spirituality. Many believe, for example, that high self-esteem is spiritually dangerous because it implies a lack of humility. In spite of the delicacy of some of the questions we discuss, we are anxious to share our views for one very important reason: they are different, and therein lies their value. This difference requires you to think about our views and understand them before accepting or rejecting them. A reflexive response based on similarity to, or difference from, prior experiences simply won't do.

Ultimately, we suggest that self-esteem and spirituality influence successful living more than any other factors. They are the "manna" of our psychological and spiritual existence during our mortal lives. They are the sum and substance of the internal man, which must be nurtured and perfected if we are to overcome the natural man within us and the corruption that surrounds us. Self-esteem and spirituality are the path of self-reliance and internal strength in governing our lives during our mortal experiences. We focus on the realities and difficulties of everyday life in cultivating spirituality and self-esteem, and we hope the reader finds our thesis clear and consistent. Successful living is successful struggling. Our own highly individualized responses to struggles — both spiritually and psychologically — teach us what we are and how to think about ourselves. This book, then, is about successful struggling, the kind of struggling that leads to high levels of spirituality and self-esteem, the two most important ingredients in perfecting the internal self.

We do not mean to imply, however, that we consider spirituality and self-esteem to be the same thing. Nothing could be further from the truth. They are distinctly separate and unique dimensions of our mortal experiences. But, paradoxically, they both seem to be influenced by remarkably similar underlying developmental processes. We explain this fascinating similarity more fully later. Before that, however, we need to provide a more complete discussion of the origins and meaning of spirituality, self-esteem, and the eternal identity. We continually emphasize truly cultivating the internal self, both spiritually and psychologically, and show the general bankruptcy of simply trying to imitate the outward manifestations of these cherished internal qualities.

Chapter Two

The Eternal Self

The concepts we are about to discuss have far-reaching implications in spite of their simplicity and directness. You see, we suggest that our eternal identity is, when properly understood, a most influential determinant of both secular and spiritual behavior. At this very moment, you are being influenced by an enduring identity that started before your mortal existence and will continue as part of you throughout your eternal existence. This internal/eternal identity is as active and alive as you are. It influences your thoughts, feelings, and perceptions. It influences everything, from how you read this book to your general disposition toward good and evil. It is not just an important part of you; it may actually be the essence of you. Learning to recognize and respond to this part of ourselves is essential to our developing both spirituality and self-esteem.

There can be little doubt that we existed prior to mortality. Many scriptures attest to this fact. The more revealing ones include Abraham 3:22–23, wherein the Lord showed Abraham "the intelligences that were organized before the world was; and among all these there were many of the noble and great ones; . . . for he stood among those that were spirits, and he saw that they were good; and he said unto me: Abraham, thou art one of them, thou wast chosen before thou wast born." In Doctrine and Covenants 49:17 the Lord discusses man's "creation before the world was made." And in Doctrine and Covenants 93:29 the Lord says, "Man was also in the beginning with God."

The message of these scriptures is clear. We all existed before we came to this earthly estate. We can also infer that there were important differences between us in that premortal existence. Abraham recognized these differences by noting that some spirits were noble and great, implying, by contrast, that there were others of lesser stature. And there is probably no more dramatic a manifestation of differences between spiritual temperaments and dispositions than a third of the hosts of heaven choosing not to follow the Savior. Bearing all this in mind, we assume that we are eternal in nature and that we were unique and different from one another in the premortal existence, just as we are unique and different from one other in mortality.

Joseph Fielding Smith gave us a concise definition of our eternal identity: "There is something called intelligence which always existed. It is the real eternal part of man, which was not created or made. *This intelligence combined with the spirit constitutes the spiritual identity or individual*" (*The Progress of Man* [Salt Lake City: Genealogical Society of Utah, 1936], p. 11; emphasis added).

Our eternal identity consists of an element that was never created (intelligence) combined with a part that was spiritually created by our Heavenly Father (spirit). These two parts compose our eternal identity, which existed before we were born and accompanied us into mortality. Our eternal identity is separate and apart, distinct and different, from any other eternal identity. It contributes to our earthly personality and is influenced by earthly experiences. It is also the enduring, fundamental self that can transcend circumstance, culture, race, genetics, or other temporal and temporary influences. It is the internal essence of what we are and of what we may become.

The concept of eternal identity is simple enough. At the core of our eternal being are dispositions and attributes that influence all we do and may even define who we are. They are certainly the source of much of our spirituality and self-esteem. The powerful implications for the development of spirituality and self-esteem that flow from this highly personalized view of man are rarely examined or understood. You see, fundamentally these implications suggest that we should turn inward to find enduring spirituality and self-esteem. Yet we live in a society that relentlessly teaches, reinforces, and occasionally demands compliance with external forces. Most of us are taught how important it is to appear appropriately calm, interested, or humble in the required way, even when we actually feel agitated, bored, or angry. But few of us are taught to turn inward to find and express our more authentic and enduring thoughts and feelings, some of which are at least partial expressions of our eternal identity.

There is a continual struggle between the internal and external influences that provide direction to our lives. Although we may wish it were not so, the evidence is undeniable that we are living in the age of the twentieth-century rational man. Computer technology, data analysis, and the underlying mentality that gives rise to sophisticated decision-making procedures prevail in all of our lives. Please don't misunderstand us on this point. We are not anti-technology. In fact, the manuscript of this book was written on an IBM computer, and we are grateful to have it. It's marvelous. But as technological sophistication increases, we suggest, it becomes progressively more difficult for us to turn inward with humility and simple faith and then respond to feelings (which can be hard to discern or understand in logical terms) when we are trying to solve complex problems. Yet that is precisely the role and function of spirituality in our lives, particularly on matters that transcend our mortal understanding. There is only one acceptable theological solution to this problem: to so perfect the internal self, the receiver and amplifer of spiritual guidance, so that we develop more faith in our capacity for spiritual guidance than in the technology that surrounds us. Cultivating and developing our internal/eternal identity is spiritual growth and development.

Alienating the Internal/Eternal Self: The Dangers of Imitation

There are many ways we can alienate ourselves from the influence of our internal/eternal identity. One of them is particularly subtle and dangerous because we live in a world of powerful external social influences and incentives. As children we are carefully tutored in the art of being socially appropriate, socially acceptable, and gaining the approval of others, particularly our parents. Generally speaking, we are taught to gain this approval by learning how to please — to imitate what we think others most want us to be. Examples of this process are numerous. It's the high-performing high school athlete or straight-A student eager for the approving smile of a loving mom or dad. In later years, it's the thriving young executive who imitates corporate leaders in dress, speech, and values because these are seen as essential ingredients for a successful career.

All of these socialization processes are perfectly natural and healthy unless they are overdone. Then they become quite dangerous. You see, elements in the process of learning to please others are the very elements that, when *abused*, help create two significant barriers to successful living:

1. Conformity and compliance in exchange for social approval, and

2. Disregard for the internal self as a source of personal direction and approval.

Neither of these two conditions can foster the development of our temporal or eternal well-being. Yet the practice of surrendering the direction of our lives to influences external to ourselves has become so accepted that we barely even notice how willing we are to do so. And the damage we do is frightening as soon as we start noticing its effects. Our sensitivity to what is truly inside of us is gradually eroded away and replaced by a willingness to be what will bring us the rewards and approval of the culture that surrounds us. As the "public" self grows stronger, the "private" self withers away. Under these conditions both children and adults are most easily moved by the winds of fickle fads, fashions, and friends. External appearances compete with internal substance and external influences clash with internal influences in shaping and developing both our secular and our spiritual identities.

Enduring happiness and contentment can come only from attending to the internal/eternal identity and fostering it. That identity is the self that is in tune with what we were before the world was and what we can be after the world passes away. That unique self will flourish when spirituality and self-esteem are nurtured. Under those conditions, external behavior becomes the spontaneous expression of our internal/eternal nature.

Of course, the question of paramount concern is how to increase our awareness of our internal/eternal nature while living in a world that is so externally oriented. In the context of internal authenticity, self-approval rings synonymous with approval from the Lord when our thoughts and actions are motivated by our Christlike inclinations. Long gone is the influence of such mortal-pleasing motives as those of the scribes and Pharisees, who were "like unto whited sepulchres, which indeed appear beautiful outward, but are within full of dead men's bones, and of all uncleanness" (Matthew 23:27).

Chapter Three

Spirituality: What It Is, Where It Comes From, and What It Does

Confusion between external appearances and internal substance is everywhere, even in some of our most cherished ideas about spirituality and self-esteem. The challenge before us is to discriminate carefully between enduring inward spirituality and self-esteem and their imitative outward forms. As you might guess, distinguishing between them can be difficult. Spirituality and self-esteem are such highly prized qualities that we unwittingly imitate their outward appearance in hopes of gaining the happiness that only their internal presence can provide. So, although the external appearance of spirituality or self-esteem may look the same as its internal substance, it is not the same. To resist the attractive allure of hollow imitations, we must accurately understand what the essential properties of spirituality and self-esteem are and why we are so easily influenced by external appearances.

The presence of such internal substance as spirituality and self-esteem is usually inferred from such external behavior as attending church, paying tithes, or appearing self-confident.

There is an almost reflexive tendency to consider spirituality *to be* attending church or paying tithes, and to consider self-esteem *to be* appearing self-confident. In fact, "too often we think of the spiritual life as something that can be *had*, an invisible equivalent to our material possessions. We think of . . . spiritual practices like meditation as "techniques" that stamp out saints like an assembly line produces shoes" (Robert Ellwood, "The Paradox of the Pathless Path," *American Theosophist*, 15 Nov. 1987, vol. 75, no. 10).

But all spiritual behaviors are not necessarily an expression of a charitable heart or of self-esteem. Remember, *what* we see people do does not necessarily indicate *why* they do it. The very same positive behavior of paying tithes can be prompted by many different motives, which can be either positive or negative—humility and gratitude, or fear and guilt. To truly recognize spirituality and self-esteem, then, we must take more notice of their private, internal manifestations while recognizing external behavior as a natural by-product of these essential traits—as they were always intended to be.

For example, a speaker stands at the pulpit, smiling as the congregation laughs at his clever joke. He proceeds in a deep and convincing voice to expound on various doctrines. He concludes with great sincerity and conviction. After the meeting, people shake his hand, complimenting him for a highly motivating talk from someone who is obviously self-assured and spiritual. As he leaves the chapel, he says to himself, "I followed my script. I made them laugh. I spoke in my deepest voice. I tried to look sincere. People seemed convinced. I must have given a good talk."

Would you rate this person high on spirituality or self-esteem? He certainly filled his assignment well. But our observations tell us more about his competence as an orator than about his spirituality or his self-esteem. What do you think? Is he high in spirituality or self-esteem?

Actually, he may well rate low in both qualities. We suggest that his spirituality is in doubt because he lacks humility and simple authenticity in his delivery. He gave a good performance, but genuine spirituality can seldom be packaged in a well-rehearsed delivery.

His self-esteem is equally doubtful. Even though he is singing his own praises to himself, his self-approval is intimately linked to the approval he receives from others. How much one needs the approval of others is a most revealing indicator of low self-esteem. This speaker, like so many of us, played the part of someone with high self-esteem as a means of defending against his very lack of it.

The congregation saw the typical trappings of assumed spirituality and high self-esteem: inspiring phrases, poignant pauses, self-assurance, quick wit, forceful voice, and so forth. In this case, however, the trappings do not represent the real thing. Instead, the behavior was like the wrapping paper on a present. Even though we call a brightly wrapped box a present, it really is not. The present is inside the box. (If you think we're splitting hairs, try convincing your children next Christmas that the colorful box with the shiny bow *is* their present, even though it's empty!) In the same way, our speaker hoped to become someone with spirituality and high self-esteem by wrapping himself up in the pretty paper and beautiful bows of spiritual, self-assured behavior, when in fact his character was empty.

What Is Spirituality?

Before we can discuss spirituality, we need to have a shared understanding of what it is. Fortunately, the scriptures provide us a clear picture. Elder Dallin H. Oaks notes the consistency with which the scriptures refer to the heart when discussing or portraying spirituality. The heart, as we shall see, is a metaphor representing the capacity to sense and then respond to the spiritual dimension that surrounds and pervades our mortal existence. Elder Oaks cites several examples of the heart representing spirituality (see *Pure in Heart* [Salt Lake City: Bookcraft, 1988], pp. 114–15):

1. "When the prophet Samuel anointed Saul to be king over Israel, 'God gave [Saul] another heart' (1 Samuel 10:9)."

2. When Nephi was caught in intense conflict with Laman and Lemuel, he "wrote that he was 'grieved because of the hardness of their hearts' (1 Nephi 15:4)."

3. "After Alma the Younger was converted, he described spirituality in terms of a change of heart. He said that his father preached to the people, and 'they awoke unto God' (Alma 5:7) and 'a mighty change was also wrought in their hearts' (Alma 5:13)."

4. Alma "asked the people of his day a question that can serve as a measure of spirituality in any day or time: 'And now behold, I ask of you, my brethren of the church, have ye spiritually been born of God? Have ye received his image in your countenances? Have ye experienced this mighty change in your hearts?' (Alma 5:14)."

5. "Helaman declares that 'faith and repentance bringeth a change of heart' (Helaman 15:7)."

6. In the book of Helaman, Mormon "describes a people whose faith in Christ filled their souls with joy and consolation, 'yea, even to the purifying and the sanctification of their hearts, which sanctification cometh because of their yielding their hearts unto God' (Helaman 3:35)."

7. Mormon describes "the opposite of spirituality as a hardness of heart. Thus, in the book of Ether we read: 'But behold, the Spirit of the Lord had ceased striving with them, and Satan had full power over the hearts of the people; for they were given up unto the hardness of their hearts, and the blindness of their minds' (Ether 15:19)."

8. Nephi tells us "in the Book of Mormon, 'Behold, there

are many that harden their hearts against the Holy Spirit, that it hath no place in them' (2 Nephi 33:2)."

When the heart, or our spiritual nature, is hardened or ignored, our sensitivity to discern and understand spiritual things is crippled. When the heart is softened or changed, our ability to recognize eternal truth and its source is enhanced, and we humbly acknowledge and worship that source. The heart, or spirituality, defines the righteous soul and the spiritual essence of our eternal identity.

From this discussion, we can conclude some things about, first, what spirituality is not, and, then, about what spirituality is.

What Spirituality Is NOT

Even though spirituality is something we are aware of and can think about, it is NOT merely an idea, a concept, or a thought.

Even though spirituality has many behavioral manifestations, spirituality is NOT simply the behaviors that are frequently associated with righteous living.

Even though spirituality is something we experience primarily through our emotions, it is NOT just a feeling or an emotion in the world's meaning.

What Spirituality IS

Spirituality IS our capacity to experience, understand, and respond to the spiritual dimension of life that surrounds us.

Spirituality IS experiencing God's divine nature and, as a result of that experience, finding our sensitivity to and our capacity for love, charity, and compassion are increased beyond natural capacity.

Spirituality IS sensitivity to the promptings of the Holy Ghost, which guide and direct our lives toward spiritual purposes that transcend the wisdom of the natural man.

Spirituality IS the direct expression of our spiritual nature (eternal identity) as we gradually immunize ourselves against the sin and corruption of the natural world we live in.

Spirituality is not a secular event, even though it takes place in a secular world. Regrettably, however, secular and spiritual events are often confused with each other. That is not surprising. Spiritual events always occur in a secular context. That is why it is so easy to confuse authentic spiritual experiences with the behavior that most frequently occurs with them. The presence of intense emotions provides a good example. Weeping frequently accompanies such spiritual events as the bearing of testimonies. The weeping itself is not a spiritual event. Nevertheless, because it is such a typical reaction to spiritual manifestations, many people confuse the two. But the tears are not the testimony.

This point is extremely important. Often we suppose that an authentic spiritual experience is taking place when we see the outward secular rituals that accompany it. For instance, many will say that daily scripture reading is a spiritual activity. Actually, it is a secular activity that may or may not yield spiritual benefits. An obsessive ritual of daily scripture reading to satisfy a handbook of instructions for righteous living is not likely to be performed in a spirit that invites the Spirit. But reading the scriptures daily while humbly recognizing the need for spiritual sustenance and working patiently for spiritual improvement is another matter entirely. That is not an empty ritual. And for precisely that reason, the secular activity of reading the scriptures may be blessed by the presence of the Spirit. Truman Madsen eloquently describes such spiritual events (note how each is by no means a description of an outward behavior):

"Prayer flashes, when our words outreach thought and we seem to be listening above ourselves, completely at home while we are surprised at hints of hidden spirit memories within.

"*Familiarity of persons,* immediate luminous rapport — this face or that gesture or motion — that elicits the sense of recall, a premortal intimacy, especially in the environs of teaching and being taught.

"*Haunting sensations,* usually visual, sometimes auditory, of a landscape of life or a bitter predicament in the soul, that call up simultaneous feelings of 'again' and 'for the first time'; like being thrust, as leading actor, into the last act of a play without knowing, and yet almost knowing, what occurred in the first two.

"*Numbing protests* from below sometimes of unrelievable urgency or guilt, that are ruthless in unmasking our pretense. These are not simply the yeas or nays of 'conscience' about acts, but bell sounds of a whole self that will not be muffled, that ring with presentiments, thrusting us toward ends that seem tied to an elusive but white-lighted blueprint inside.

"*Shades of consciousness* that occur just at awakening or just before sleep, unpredictably impressing while they express, in images or silent words or free association. By the sanctity of their feeling-tone, these are different than our usual helter-skelter menagerie of thought.

"*Dreams and illusions* that seem not to be mere dreams or mere illusions, catching us quite off-guard and lingering in their after-effect, as if life were a game of internal hide-the-thimble and we were 'getting warm' to our own potential.

"*Unaccountable reverberations* (e.g. in tear-filled eye or tingling throat or spine) from a phrase or sentiment (which, for the speaker or writer may be merely parenthetical), or from a strain of music, or some trivial stimulus in the midst of drudgery, bearing a holy atmosphere of spontaneous and total recognition.

"*Reflection of our faces* in the mirror when we look in and not just at, our eyes. As if light were coming to the surface, and a curious recovery, and even awe, of the self occurs. There lurks an autobiography, a soul-story that is foreign, yet intimate, unfolding a more-than-I-thought-I-was.

"*Right-track feelings*, the sense of the foreordained, like emerging from a fever to find that roughshod or happenstance trials have been presided over by some uncanny instinctual self who knows what he is about. Just before or just after turning a crucial corner, this someone nearer than you, that *is* you, holds a quiet celebration that injects peace into the marrow of the bones.

"Such flashes and drives are tied to the whole gamut of complex mental life and may have neat and utterly mundane naturalistic explanations (such as the chemistry of the occipital lobe). Yet the joy that comes from these uprisings, rooted, as they seem to be, in some more primal creative being and that, in turn, in God, supersedes any of the pleasures of human possession or external manipulation" (*Eternal Man* [Salt Lake City: Deseret Book Co., 1966], pp. 75–76).

Origins of Spirituality

Humility is a concept that plays an essential role in the origins of spirituality. Naturally, there are other important considerations, but the scriptures are clear and consistent on two points regarding humility and spirituality. First, the absence of humility virtually precludes the development of spirituality. And, second, the presence of humility is essential for spiritual growth.

We find in Alma 32 what could well be the most penetrating discussion of faith and its development in the standard works. This chapter gives us the blueprint for developing spirituality. The role of humility in that process is paramount. Alma preaches to the poor and afflicted who were cast out of their own synagogues because of their extreme poverty. When Alma sees that the people are penitent and that their afflictions have truly humbled them, he explains: "It is because that ye are cast out, that ye are despised of your brethren because of your exceeding poverty, that ye are brought to a lowliness of heart; for ye are necessarily brought to be humble. And now, because ye are compelled to be humble blessed are ye; for a man sometimes, if he is compelled to be humble, seeketh repentance. . . . Yea, he that truly humbleth himself, and repenteth of his sins, and endureth to the end, the same shall be blessed" (Alma 32:12–13, 15).

We can find at least three important points in Alma's words:

1. Affliction can lead to humility for the proud, and spiritual knowledge and understanding can lead to humility for the teachable.

2. Humility leads to repentance.

3. Humility and repentance are necessary for getting close to God.

The message could not be clearer: humility is essential to spiritual growth. And though many different factors may contribute to humility, two of the more important ones are spiritual knowledge and understanding, and afflictions and hardship.

We can only speculate about why humility seems to pose such a difficult problem for most of us during our mortal existence. Maybe it's just a hard attribute to cultivate in a well-educated and affluent society. The scriptures certainly suggest that the wealthy and the well-educated are likely to have a difficult time with humility. But most of us understand that in this life we are expected to learn how to discern good from evil and respond to them correctly. Perhaps our individual struggle with pride and humility is one of the better indicators of just how well we are doing at discerning and responding to good and evil in our own lives.

The essence of pride is self-aggrandizement, a condition that could not be more irrelevant to the task of preparing ourselves to be with Deity. Nothing else distracts us more completely from becoming like our Heavenly Father. Satan wanted to rule over us in a self-aggrandizing way, but Christ wanted to serve us. In so doing, He shunned short-term self-interests in favor of the long-term selfless act of atoning for the sins of all mankind. And during that atonement, at the moment of his greatest anguish, the humble heart of our Savior was evident in his contrite words, "Not my will, but thine, be done" (Luke 22:42). Pride was not there, nor could it have been. It is this attribute of humility that we must seek after and acquire.

Clearly, we know more about the consequences of pride than we know of its origin. Those consequences could not be more sobering. For example, the scriptures teach us that in the last days when the earth is cleansed by burning, the proud shall be as stubble (see 3 Nephi 25:1; D&C 29:9; D&C 64:24). The Lord has specifically warned his servants: "Beware of pride, lest thou shouldst enter into temptation" (D&C 23:1) and "thou shalt not be proud in thy heart" (D&C 42:40).

The rewards for humility are equally clear and profound. Two compelling examples are in the Doctrine and Covenants. "Inasmuch as you strip yourselves from jealousies and fears, and humble yourselves before me, . . . the veil shall be rent and you shall see me and know that I am—not with the carnal neither natural mind, but with the spiritual" (D&C 67:10). "My Spirit is sent forth into the world to enlighten the humble and contrite, and to the condemnation of the ungodly" (D&C 136:33).

The Lord wishes us to free ourselves from the myopic concerns of personal pride. The reasons are obvious. We must each undergo an internally motivated cleansing, in which we recognize our pride and choose to expunge it from our soul. When this task has proven too difficult for some of his people, the Lord has given them external motivation to more fully understand their vulnerability and their ultimate lack of self-sufficiency. Afflictions and hardships are not conditions in which pride is most likely to thrive.

Surely it would be difficult to underplay the importance of humility in the development of spirituality. Genuine humility is the outward expression of the internal state of the soul. Its essence is gratitude and appreciation for Deity's benevolent care and concern for us. That's the internal part. Its external manifestations will include our benevolent care and concern for others. Such activities manifest the spiritual essence of our eternal identity, which is most fully liberated by humility in the otherwise natural man.

Please notice carefully, however, that neither spirituality nor humility is behavior that is motivated by social customs, conformity, seeking the approval of others, or pretending to be better than we actually are. Humility and its resulting spirituality are internal events whose real qualities cannot be imitated, even though its outward appearances can.

Consequences of Spirituality

We may have become so accustomed to hearing the profound concepts and doctrines that teach us the consequences of spirituality that we have forgotten their deep meaning. They tell us that the development of spirituality is the most noble aspiration of human experience. And, as it develops, its consequences will be equally noble. Spirituality is an inner framework through which we view life, value life, and live life. To the spiritually minded, the meaning and value of daily activities are found through the enlarged perspective of spiritual understanding. Paul's letter to the Romans makes this clear:

"For they that are after the flesh do mind the things of the flesh; but they that are after the Spirit the things of the Spirit. For to be carnally minded is death; but to be spiritually minded is life and peace" (Romans 8:5–6).

Authentic spirituality is a sharp blade that cuts incisively into the resistant fabric of secular views and values. The importance of accomplishments and possessions starts to fade when we come to spiritually understand our Savior, the Atonement, and the underlying purpose of life. Tithes are paid out of a deep understanding of the purpose of the Lord's kingdom and a firm commitment to building it. The opportunity to "share" and "serve" is gratefully accepted instead of begrudgingly endured. Tolerance for others increases naturally as the spiritual heart melts away the emotional scars of unfulfilled living and personal frustration. Authentic spirituality inevitably becomes the prime determinant of priorities and choices. What we "want" to do becomes what we "ought" to do. Self-coercion is no longer necessary. Choices become an automatic and natural extension of what we experience and understand spiritually.

Because spirituality is internal, it cannot be seen. Nevertheless, we can see many of its influences. Authentic spirituality shows in our words, our attitudes, and our behaviors. But unlike false appearances of spirituality, all of these indicators actually are more Christlike because the behavior is now rooted in genuine spiritual motives.

Chapter Four

Self-Esteem: What It Is, Where It Comes From, and What It Does

The importance of self-esteem to emotional well-being is undeniable. The degree to which we find contentment and happiness in life is in large measure determined by our level of self-esteem. Yet, like so many other important personal attributes, self-esteem seems to be as elusive as it is important.

The Paradox of Self-Esteem

For the most part, high levels of outward success are accompanied by equally high levels of inward distress. This puzzling paradox suggests that the self-esteem we so vigorously seek in external things is not to be found there. Recent statistics show an ever-increasing incidence of emotional and mental difficulties in a population that, judging by its standard of living and its accomplishments, should be experiencing an ever-increasing sense of contentment and satisfaction. This paradoxical sense of dissatisfaction is typified by the statement of a seventy-year-old man reflecting on his life's work: "[My] whole life has been a succession of disappointments. I can scarcely recollect a single instance of success in anything that I ever undertook" (as quoted in John F. Kennedy, *Profiles in Courage* [New York: Harper, 1956], p. 35).

These words were not uttered by a person whose life was fraught with failure and a lack of distinction as the speaker would have us believe. On the contrary, this seventy-year-old gentleman was John Quincy Adams, congressman, senator, ambassador to foreign countries, and sixth president of the United States. Few others had greater influence on the direction of this country. How could anyone with a lifetime of such apparent achievements and honors be so self-deprecating?

John Quincy Adams is by no means unique in his ability to disregard his successes and dwell upon his failures. Our own day is filled with examples of this frustrating psychological treadmill upon which a variety of individuals plod but never gain any emotional ground. Completing an education, keeping a job, finding a mate, maintaining significant relationships, and raising a family have never been more difficult or required more competence to accomplish successfully. And people do succeed. Yet, in the face of compelling evidence that people's successes typically outweigh their failures, an abundance of these same people, like John Quincy Adams, suffer from chronic low self-esteem.

We must ask ourselves if the trappings of a successful life — financial security, position in profession and community, family and friends, in fact, the very things we have been told we should work toward — do not bring us that elusive sense of contentment, then where else do we look? Just where self-esteem originates and how we can consciously develop it are the intriguing questions we examine next.

Traditional Views of Self-Esteem

Most theories of the origin of self-esteem suggest that how we feel about ourselves is determined in large part by how we are seen by significant others. According to these theories, the more we are loved and appreciated by parents, peers, and spouses, the more we will love and appreciate ourselves. Under conditions where the social environment is so reinforcing, it is assumed that the individual will grow to have high self-esteem.

Although the way that others perceive us does contribute to our self-esteem, we see little reason to rely solely on external influences to understand the origins of self-esteem for either children or adults. Common sense and our experience as ecclesiastical leaders and clinicians have led us to believe that high or low levels of self-esteem can be the result of events that have nothing to do with professional or social success or with the way in which we are thought of by significant others.

According to most theories, then, children who have had kind, affectionate parents would have obvious and unquestioning self-confidence. Children who were raised by harsh, uncaring parents would accept their belittling criticisms as truth, believing themselves to be only as good as their parents say they are. Yet experience has taught us otherwise. We have seen individuals who had abusive, traumatic childhoods who are still happy, productive, and self-confident adults; we have seen others who grew up in supportive, nurturing environments who nevertheless suffer from debilitating self-doubts and low self-esteem. These observations suggest that more is involved in the development of high or low self-esteem than what psychology calls "external social learning factors."

What Is Self-Esteem?

We have already characterized self-esteem as internal well-being. It is an appreciation for the self that is more a feeling than a belief. It is a sense of emotional security that allows us to function more fully, freely, and effectively in almost every facet of life. We have already noted that the absence of self-esteem has repeatedly been demonstrated to impair human functioning in ways far too numerous to give a full account of here. Its devastating effects are consistent regardless of social class, levels of achievement, or religious affiliation. Its positive effects are equally clear and consistent.

Unlike most theories, which assert that the approval of others is one of the prime ingredients in self-esteem, we suggest that an adult's self-esteem does not depend upon the approval or praise of others. Rather, an adult's self-esteem is based on an internal process of being aware of, paying attention to, and fully experiencing the internal emotional consequences of our own behavior. Our own feelings about our behavior is the substance from which our self-esteem either grows or withers.

But our self-evaluative feelings are not random or arbitrary. Underlying specific behavior patterns are attributes that actually create positive and negative psychological experiences (Bednar, et al., 1989). Three terms are central to this concept of self-esteem: *coping, avoidance,* and *self-evaluations.*

Coping

Coping requires a candid and forthright facing up to things that we fear. It is a way of looking at ourselves and being honest about ourselves with others. It means we have both the willingness and the strength to acknowledge the things that are wrong with us. We don't hide from the painful things that we know are true about ourselves. Instead, we recognize them and take responsibility for them.

Coping is the path of insight, reality testing, honesty, personal growth, and development. It involves two types of psychological risk: first, the risk of truly knowing ourselves and, second, the risk of truly being known by others. Risk-taking allows us to face and overcome problems in spite of the pain they create. A willingness to cope with difficult problems is

35

the cardinal characteristic of emotionally healthy people. It is also an essential element in the development of personal self-esteem.

Avoidance

Avoidance is denying, distorting, and rationalizing the negative things we don't care to face about ourselves or others. It is an attempt to avoid acknowledging and taking ownership of the problems we face because of the pain and distress involved. The denial and distortions inherent in the process of avoidance allow us to try to look at things the way we would like them to be rather than the way they really are. This relatively primitive type of psychological response is associated with emotional problems, low self-esteem, and the absence of psychological growth and development. It is also a major element in virtually all theories of disordered human behavior.

Self-Evaluations

The psychological characteristics inherent in *coping* and *avoidance* are qualitatively different. Avoidance is basically a form of denial and an escape from conflict that requires distortions of thinking and perception. These psychological responses are inherently inadequate responses to conflict. We cannot think of any enduring benefits to be derived by consistently avoiding conflict situations as a way of containing the unpleasant experience of fear and anxiety.

On the other hand, coping is a means by which we can acquire a more accurate understanding of self and others. Coping involves facing conflict realistically, learning how to tolerate the distress inherent in conflict situations, and gradually modifying the personality through mature conflict resolution. The underlying qualities that sustain a coping response are socially valued and essential ingredients in personal and interpersonal problem-solving.

The self-evaluative processes are based on continually noticing, monitoring, thinking about, and directly experiencing the emotional consequences of our more enduring patterns of behavior. All behavior patterns contain varying degrees and mixtures of our enduring tendency to avoid or to cope with conflict. We suggest that self-evaluations tend to be consistently negative in the presence of patterns of avoidance simply because avoidance responses are intrinsically inadequate and unflattering. Conversely, favorable self-evaluations are the inevitable result of coping. Inherent in the coping responses are higher levels of risk-taking, personal responsibility, and human growth, all of which are inherently affirming psychological experiences. In brief, favorable self-evaluations tend to accompany coping because of the favorable qualities inherent in coping responses; unfavorable self-evaluations tend to accompany avoidance because of the unfavorable qualities inherent in avoidance responses. So, you see, it is our own, self-generated approval or disapproval that determines our own level of self-esteem.

Although self-evaluations are the most important determinants of self-esteem, the feedback of others, or what we call the social environment, influences how we feel about ourselves. We would like to examine this social environment (external feedback) and its potential influence on self-evaluations (internal feedback) in terms of four assumptions. These assumptions explain the two sources of feedback that play a role in developing our self-esteem.

Assumption 1: Everyone should expect to receive regular amounts of negative feedback from the social environment, most of which is probably valid. At first this assumption may sound harsh by implying that we are the worthy recipients of punishing criticism, but we are not suggesting that we really are as incompetent and lowly as the negative social feedback might sound. Many people, however, believe that a person can have high self-esteem only in a world where criticism does not exist or can be easily dismissed as inaccurate. That belief is obviously false. Such a world does not exist.

Why, then, is criticism or other negative feedback an inevitable reality for us all? Basically, we are all different from one another. The differences result in our naturally gravitating to others who are most similar to ourselves. Groups are formed, by intent or by default, to meet human needs. How that is accomplished varies from one group to another. Each group and, indeed, individuals within the group, have preconceived ideas and opinions about what is acceptable or desirable behavior within the group. Because such notions can vary within the group as well as between different groups, it is unreasonable to assume that any one person can be found acceptable by every group she or he comes in contact with or wishes to belong to. At some point, we all will be found unacceptable by one group or another.

Another, more subtle form of negative feedback is hidden or mixed messages. Often appearing as compliments, such messages will leave you wondering, "Just exactly what did he mean by that?" We've all heard such compliments as, "My, you look good *today*," implying that usually we don't look good or, "That outfit makes you look much thinner," suggesting that we're overweight. Depending upon our individual sensitivity to criticism, possibilities for disconfirming feedback can loom large. Negative feedback, which may be valid from the speaker's point of view, is an everyday fact of life.

Assumption 2: Most people receive and enjoy substantial amounts of authentic favorable social feedback but tend not to believe it. The second assumption is a regrettable consequence of the first. If we view negative feedback as a potential threat of rejection and therefore something to be avoided, *impression management* may result. Impression management is the process of being something you aren't in order to avoid the perceived threat of rejection. Impression management may take the form of adopting others' speech, dress, ideas, and so forth, pretending to be knowledgeable and interested in subjects you know nothing about, rejecting values that the group criticizes, or remaining silent out of fear of contradicting what everybody else thinks.

Impression management results in two adverse conditions. First, individuals become progressively alienated from what they really think and feel, making it increasingly difficult for them to be genuine. Second, when valid, positive feedback is offered, individuals don't accept it, fearing that the feedback is directed to the false image they have presented rather than to the true self inside. Frequently such individuals reply, "If you really knew me, you wouldn't say such nice things."

Assumption 3: Self-evaluations are a psychological reality for most people. Research shows that beginning at approximately age six to eight, we observe and evaluate our own behavior. The process has both cognitive (thinking) and affective (feeling) aspects. If our own evaluation of a performance is positive, we experience affirming emotions towards the self. If our evaluations are negative, we experience disconfirming emotions about ourselves. As both actor and spectator of our behaviors *and* thoughts, we have front-row seats to witness our own avoiding or coping with psychological threats, which actions produce negative or positive self-evaluations, respectively.

Assumption 4: Self-evaluations provide continuous affective feedback from the self about the adequacy of the self. The fourth assumption reveals the importance of self-evaluations as the primary source of self-esteem. Self-esteem is not primarily a thought but a subjective and enduring state of self-approval. If we evaluate what we do in a positive way, we experience affirming emotions of greater confidence or acceptance toward the self. If we evaluate what we do in a negative way, we experience emotions that may range from a sense of inadequacy and helplessness to utter self-contempt.

The level of self-esteem indicates the degree to which life events will be stressful. If the level of self-esteem is high, the level of personal stress will be correspondingly low. On the other hand, if the level of self-esteem is low, the level of personal stress will be high.

The characteristics associated with high levels of self-esteem — risk-taking, responsibility, and confidence — all contribute to minimizing stress. Levels of stress as affected by self-esteem will dictate the personal response style we adopt when confronted by stress. With low self-esteem and high stress, we adopt an avoidant style. With high self-esteem and low levels of stress, we adopt a coping style.

The personal response style generates self-evaluations that vary from favorable to unfavorable. Self-evaluations generate internal feedback, which takes the form of self-generated approval or self-generated disapproval. The nature of the internal feedback then affects the level of self-esteem.

External feedback, although not as important or as potent a contributing factor, also affects self-esteem. Credible positive feedback is believable and favorable. Credible negative feedback is believable and unfavorable. Uncredible feedback can be either positive or negative but is discounted by the person receiving it.

SELF-EVALUATION FORM

This exercise will help you evaluate yourself in terms of three attributes that are associated with individuals who possess high levels of self-esteem: risk-taking, responsibility, and confidence. Before you start the exercise, review the definitions of these three attributes:

Risk-taking   The willingness to declare your thoughts and feelings without knowing how they will be received by others. The less you know about how they will be received, the greater the risk. It is the risk of being known as you really are.

Responsibility   The willingness to take ownership of the causes and consequences of your behavior. You acknowledge your role in what you do and the effect it has on you and on others.

Confidence   Faith in yourself—the ability to deal comfortably with potential stress, uncertainty, or embarrassment without arrogance or conceit.

With these definitions in mind, rate the degree to which you typically demonstrate risk-taking, responsibility, and confidence in the following situations. Remember, there are no right or wrong answers, only self-evaluations of your own behavior.

Instructions: Circle the number that most closely reflects your self-evaluation in each category.

1. You are out with a group of friends. How much risk-taking, responsibility, and confidence do you show when the group is deciding what movie they will see or at what restaurant they will eat?

	Little				*A lot*
Risk-taking:	1	2	3	4	5
Responsibility:	1	2	3	4	5
Confidence:	1	2	3	4	5

2. You are talking with your spouse or partner. A topic you have strong feelings about arises, such as money, sex, or

the future of your relationship. How much risk-taking, responsibility, and confidence do you show during the course of the discussion?

	Little				A lot
Risk-taking:	1	2	3	4	5
Responsibility:	1	2	3	4	5
Confidence:	1	2	3	4	5

3. You are at a large meeting, perhaps work, PTA, church, or a social gathering. Someone says something you totally disagree with. How much risk-taking, responsibility, and confidence do you show when differing opinions are asked for?

	Little				A lot
Risk-taking:	1	2	3	4	5
Responsibility:	1	2	3	4	5
Confidence:	1	2	3	4	5

4. You have just made a serious mistake at work, or with a neighbor, or with your spouse or partner. How much risk-taking, responsibility, and confidence do you show in admitting the mistake to yourself and others?

	Little				A lot
Risk-taking:	1	2	3	4	5
Responsibility:	1	2	3	4	5
Confidence:	1	2	3	4	5

5. Someone does or says something that causes you to feel such strong feelings as love, anger, happiness, or sorrow.

How much risk-taking, responsibility, and confidence do you show in expressing how you feel?

	Little				*A lot*
Risk-taking:	1	2	3	4	5
Responsibility:	1	2	3	4	5
Confidence:	1	2	3	4	5

6. Someone asks you to do a favor or take on an assignment that you would just as soon not do. How much risk-taking, responsibility, and confidence do you show in responding to the request?

	Little				*A lot*
Risk-taking:	1	2	3	4	5
Responsibility:	1	2	3	4	5
Confidence:	1	2	3	4	5

7. You begin a new job where your usual style of dress does not fit an unwritten but obvious dress code. How much risk-taking, responsibility, and confidence do you show as you adapt to your new surroundings?

	Little				*A lot*
Risk-taking:	1	2	3	4	5
Responsibility:	1	2	3	4	5
Confidence:	1	2	3	4	5

8. You are at a restaurant where the medium-rare steak you ordered turns out to be medium-well done. How much risk-taking, responsibility, and confidence do you show when the waiter returns to fill your glass with water?

	Little				*A lot*
Risk-taking:	1	2	3	4	5
Responsibility:	1	2	3	4	5
Confidence:	1	2	3	4	5

9. You find out that one of your co-workers, neighbors, or ward members is criticizing you behind your back. How much risk-taking, responsibility, and confidence do you show in dealing with the situation?

	Little				*A lot*
Risk-taking:	1	2	3	4	5
Responsibility:	1	2	3	4	5
Confidence:	1	2	3	4	5

10. Your brother is wild about his new fiancée, but you don't think the marriage will work. How much risk-taking, responsibility, and confidence do you show when considering the happiness of your brother?

	Little				*A lot*
Risk-taking:	1	2	3	4	5
Responsibility:	1	2	3	4	5
Confidence:	1	2	3	4	5

11. Review your ratings of how much risk-taking, responsibilities, and confidence you have shown in the first ten questions. Write down what you think your ratings tell you about yourself:

_____

_____

_____

_____

_____

12. How do you *feel* about what your ratings tell you about yourself?

_____

_____

_____

_____

_____

13. Go back and answer questions 1 through 12 as if you were exactly like the kind of person you really wanted to be. Compare your first answers to your second answers. What stops you from becoming the kind of person you'd like to be?

_____

_____

_____

_____

_____

Conclusion

We conclude this chapter with a modern-day parable that illustrates the relationship among the internal/eternal identity, spirituality, and self-esteem. Based on a true story, this parable clearly demonstrates the damage to both spirituality and self-esteem of catering to external influences at the expense of the internal self. This modern-day parable is related to the biblical parable of the ten virgins. The usual interpretation of the biblical parable relates to being prepared, but we suggest that it has a further message as well. Although the lamps of the ten virgins seemed identical, only five contained the crucial oil that gave off the light that would greet the groom at his coming. The other five lamps had the appearance of substance but were found empty at the moment they were to be lit. That crucial moment required the virgins to reveal the value of their respective lamps. The results of relying on outward appearance versus relying on inward substance is both clear and undeniable. Here, then, is our story.

Bill wanted to succeed. Like many of us, he measured his success by promotions at work, positions at church, and recognition from his community. He learned early that following prescribed ways of doing things would enhance his ability to achieve the success he so greatly desired. He dressed like his boss. He arrived early and stayed late, not because his responsibilities required him to, but because his boss was impressed. He second-guessed at every turn what his supervisor liked, and his work reflected that homogeneity. Each word he wrote, each task he performed, was designed with one thing in mind: promotion.

At church, he made sure his family was early so they could sit on the front row to be seen. He never declined an assignment and volunteered at every opportunity. He got his home teaching done before the second week of the month and made sure he reported that way. In Sunday School, his comments sounded impressive, although to the discerning listener, somewhat standard and not quite on the mark. Each charitable act and each manifestation of activity was designed with one thing in mind: position.

In his civic duties the same pattern emerged: prescribed behavior motivated by gain and advancement — and the formula worked well. He was promoted at work. He was given a position in church, and he was recognized for his contributions to the community. By conforming to his external environment, he was rewarded. Premeditated outward appearance gave him what he had learned to want and seek. The more he was rewarded, the more conforming he became. The more conforming he became, the more he required the external reward, because without it he felt empty inside. Something deep down inside of Bill told him that *he* was not being rewarded: it was really his formula for an immaculate outward appearance that was getting all the praise.

Then something happened. Bill began his routine in his new promotion at work, his new position at church, his elevated status in the community, but for some reason the expected reinforcement didn't come. His boss needed original and creative thinking, which Bill couldn't provide. His church leaders needed spiritual sensitivity, which Bill couldn't demonstrate. And the community got tired of seeing Bill sitting on the dais at every banquet and meeting. With the external approval withdrawn, Bill became lonely, disillusioned, and confused.

Bill's story is typical of the stories of individuals who confuse outward appearance with inward substance and promote the one as the other. By no means was Bill an evil or a fundamentally dishonest person. Rather, he was the product of a society that had taught him to please and placate others as the primary way to earn reward and approval. Bill had learned that concept very well — so well, in fact, that his rituals for success ignored unique factors, internal inklings, or individual characteristics and traits. Bill's internal/eternal identity, which made him different, special, and unique, suffered under the heavy load of social acceptance. When his professional position required him to stand on his own merits, he was unable to do so. When the spiritual sensitivity that comes with a developed internal/eternal self was called upon by his leaders, he was unable to respond. When his peers demanded more of him than a high profile and he couldn't deliver, they withdrew their support. In each instance, Bill denied his internal/eternal self to gain the approval of others, which he thought would bring him the happiness he had been taught it would.

How did Bill's denial of his internal/eternal self affect his spirituality and his self-esteem? First, it was evident that his actions at church were not motivated by charitable, humble, genuinely Christlike desires. They did not reflect or enhance that part of him that existed with God and was spiritually made by him. Rather, self-aggrandizement by way of external approval and subsequent rewarding by others seemed to be his primary concern. His lack of spirituality became evident when he needed to demonstrate true spiritual sensitivity and could not. He could not exercise what he did not have. Finally, a weak internal/eternal self was the primary cause of his plummeting self-esteem, because even as he was buying in, wholesale, to the idea that pleasing others would bring success, something inside of him reacted negatively to behavior that did not reflect his real self. His inherently avoidant behavior left him with a growing emptiness and a lack of self-approval, even as he tried to fill the emptiness with increased approval from others. When his facade ultimately failed, because there was no internal self to fall back on, he was left only with a shattered perception of himself that reflected no self-approval and little self-esteem.

Whenever the internal/eternal self is ignored, spirituality and self-esteem invariably suffer. Whenever the internal/eternal self is cultivated, spirituality and self-esteem are greatly enhanced. Regardless of which direction any of us pursues, the consequences will be both clear and considerable.

Chapter Five

Integrating Spirituality and Self-Esteem

Integrating spirituality and self-esteem into patterns of successful living is an all-important consideration. Our approach focuses on the developmental processes the two share. We believe that if you get the big pieces of a puzzle in place first, then the little ones, which are at times the most difficult and cumbersome to work with, will also fall into place. So, too, in integrating spirituality and self-esteem. When the large pieces, with their similarities and their differences, are known and established, it is much easier to recognize the smaller pieces by instinct and natural inclination.

We consider spirituality and self-esteem to be the biggest pieces of a successful life. It is easy to see why spirituality is a big piece. Our very nature is spiritual. Even in this temporal world, the Lord has told us, all his laws are spiritual. Our purpose for coming to earth is ultimately spiritual. Therefore, spirituality must be taken into account in attempting to understand what constitutes successful living. Remember, *spirituality* means the capacity to experience, understand, and respond to the promptings of the Holy Ghost as well as to directly experience or understand God's divine nature. So, although spirituality can exist in a secular world, it is by no means a secular phenomenon. Without spirituality, there can be no real happiness in a secular world, only the temporary pleasures of the natural man. Successful living *is* spiritual living.

It may not be as easy to see why we think self-esteem is a large piece of the successful life. We use the term *self-esteem* to mean an internal sense of personal well-being. A psychological theory of self-esteem that is compatible with the fundamental elements of Latter-day Saint doctrine suggests that self-esteem is a result of an internal self-evaluative process. According to that view, the more we attempt to cope with difficult problems in our lives, the more self-esteem we will develop. Inherent in the very act of coping with difficult problems are behavior patterns that please humans in spite of their difficulty. Those desirable behavior patterns produce favorable self-evaluations and contribute to our self-esteem and personal growth and development. On the other hand, psychological avoidance, which is an attempt to strategically retreat from problems we don't care to face, is an inherently inadequate response to personal conflict. Avoidance responses create negative self-evaluations, low self-esteem, and impaired personal growth and development. In the final analysis, then, our level of self-esteem is determined by the quality of character we observe in ourselves when we face problems and situations we would prefer to avoid.

But what can self-esteem contribute to successful living that spirituality does not? Why do we give it such preeminent consideration? We have three primary reasons for considering self-esteem so seriously:

1. Mortality and its attendant limitations require us to understand ourselves in temporal as well as in spiritual terms. Temporal considerations that regularly influence successful living include health care, education, and financial planning, to name but a few. And many theological concepts are expressed in temporal metaphors. The second great commandment, for

example, tells us to love our neighbors as we love ourselves. That is a difficult commandment to understand or follow if we have an improvised sense of personal worth. In this way, and many others, the quality of life we experience can profoundly affect our spiritual development.

2. Even though spirituality and self-esteem are distinctly different attributes, they both guard internal well-being in their respective spheres. They both contribute to the development of our innate potential. And they both foster our ability to be internally directed and self-governing. Achieving internal well-being and reaching our eternal potential must surely be at the top of any list of goals of personal and spiritual development.

3. Not only do spirituality and self-esteem affect each other but they are the most uncluttered manifestations of our internal/eternal identity during mortality. Self-esteem and spirituality are the temporal expressions of our eternal capacity to love all things, including ourselves, and love is the highest level of human functioning. Essentially, then, spirituality and self-esteem are the two sides of the same human coin.

Spirituality and self-esteem both require self-approving behavior in order to reside within us. We cannot have a high level of spirituality or a high level of self-esteem when we behave in ways we do not approve of. Self-approval depends on humility in a spiritual plane and on coping in a secular one. Both humility and coping are cultivated through our acting congruently with our internal/eternal identity, that part of us that lived with God and learned the difference between right and wrong. Our eternal identity resonates to all that is good and shrinks from all that is bad. Even as it chose the Savior's plan in the premortal existence, so too can it direct our choices now. In that way, self-approval results from heeding that part of ourselves that receives truth directly from its eternal source. There is no greater self-approval than the self-approval that comes from doing what we know is pleasing to the Lord.

Coping results from attending to our internal self in a secular world. If we allow our internal selves to be the prime source of our external self-expression, how we behave on the outside is congruent with what we think and feel on the inside. They become one and the same. In that manner we are true to ourselves. And regardless of the difficulty, such self-honesty is a coping response that generates a great deal of self-approval. Self-approval, in turn, strengthens self-esteem. When we are proud or avoidant, we behave contrary to our internal/eternal identity. That behavior inevitably results in self-disapproval and an absence of spirituality and self-esteem.

We must acknowledge that there are certainly many individuals in this natural world who display little spirituality and at the same time display an abundance of self-esteem. That can happen because self-esteem is a secular occurrence and spirituality is not, although self-approval remains the essential process for both. Thus we can have high self-esteem and low spirituality, but we cannot have high spirituality and low self-esteem. Where humility prevails and the individual is in tune with the Spirit of the Lord, high self-approval and, consequently, high self-esteem will always prevail, regardless of any other mortal condition:

1. High spirituality implies high self-esteem.

2. High self-esteem (on a purely secular level) is independent of spirituality.

3. The process required to develop both spirituality and self-esteem is self-approval. Self-approval results from our behaving congruently with our internal/eternal identity.

Successful living, then, entails cultivating our internal/eternal identity. Success comes when the internal/eternal self is sufficiently unencumbered by mortal foibles so that spirituality and self-esteem manifest themselves both in our behavior and in the spiritual and psychological well-being they create inside us.

Similarities between Spirituality and Self-Esteem

At first it might seem incongruous to suggest that spirituality and self-esteem share many important developmental processes. After all, spirituality is a theological concept and self-esteem is a secular concept. But let's look at it another way. If spirituality were an apple and self-esteem a banana, anyone could see that they are different. Their color, shape, and size bear no resemblance. Were we to cut them open, their differences would be even more apparent. If we were to look at the processes underlying the development of these fruits, however, we would see striking similarities. Both apples and bananas grow from seeds, which produce plants, which, in turn, produce blossoms and then fruit. Soil, water, and sunlight are necessary for both to grow. Apparently, then, different fruits go through similar developmental processes.

In themselves, self-esteem and spirituality have little in common. Self-esteem consists of characteristics and attributes that create a sense of psychological well-being. Spirituality, on the other hand, transcends the psychological and satisfies our longing for spiritual sustenance, something self-esteem cannot do. Nevertheless, if we compare the developmental processes that lead to spirituality and self-esteem, we find similarities that are important, substantive, and even remarkable.

On the following page are four different sets of psychological and spiritual processes and attributes that are associated with self-affirming and self-defeating experiences.

	Psychological	Spiritual
Self-Affirming	*Coping*	*Humility*
Experiences	Introspection	Charity
	Reality testing	Gratitude
	Insight	Teachableness
	Honesty	Spirituality
Self-Defeating	*Avoidance*	*Pride*
Experiences	Fear	Selfishness
	Denial	Self-Aggrandizement
	Distortion	Self-Centeredness
	Rationalization	Self-Servingness

Coping

The process of psychological coping is based on one basic assumption: coping requires that imperfections in the self are openly and candidly acknowledged, at least to ourselves. That's right. No illusions or false beliefs are allowed. Effective coping results in our childish and immature wishes being set aside and replaced by a more mature and realistic understanding of ourselves and the world we live in. The instant we fully recognize and understand our personal faults, our possibilities for personal growth begin. Coping is the path of—

Introspection: examining what we are thinking and feeling about ourselves and about what goes on around us.

Reality testing: questioning the accuracy and completeness of our thoughts, feelings, and understanding of ourselves and what goes on around us.

Insight: learning from introspection and reality testing things that are true and undeniable about ourselves.

Personal honesty: acknowledging and accepting responsibility for what we have learned about ourselves and showing a willingness to do something about it.

All these are attributes that when properly exercised provide each of us with a deep personal knowledge of our capacity for highly effective and successful living. The following example illustrates the process of coping and the nature of its self-affirming consequences:

It had just slipped out. Again! The little word that she didn't mean to say but couldn't stop herself from saying every time someone asked her to do something: "yes." A most willing word—positive, helpful, and friendly. For Jan, though, it had become a tyrannical little monster that sank its sharklike teeth into every request thrown in her direction. Throw a bridal shower for a second cousin on your husband's side? "Why, yes." Bake seventeen dozen dream bars for the three-stake yodeling contest? "Yes, of course I will." Feed your schizophrenic Siamese cat while you vacation in Hawaii for three weeks? "Yes, thanks for asking." "Yes, yes, yes, yes, yes."

The word rolled off her tongue before her brain even knew it was gone. She didn't really want to say yes. She knew that most of the time she shouldn't have said yes. She'd push herself to do more than she could handle, and then, in a frantic bid to be everything to everybody, she'd wind up being less than what she wanted to be to herself. Oh sure, she could tell when she was genuinely needed, when her talents couldn't easily be replaced by someone else's. The times she cringed were when she agreed to do something that anybody in the civilized world could have done just as easily and just as well. It was when she did a poor job because she had spread herself too thin or when she ignored her family's needs in order to meet less important obligations that she mentally kicked herself. Apart from a thank-you for being so "special," the only thing she could count on getting was a tension headache.

Her husband was a big help. "Just say no," he'd bellow. "Just . . . say no," she'd think. "Easy for him to say." Whenever the quorum presidency called him with an assignment he didn't want to do, he never said yes. He'd lie, instead. "Gee, Bill, that sounds great. I'd really like to be there but, um . . . I've got a vacuum cleaner convention that same day at the exact same hour. Isn't that a coincidence!"

This time, when she hung up the phone after accepting another makework assignment, Jan really asked herself why *didn't* she just say no? Her first line of reasoning was as faulty as it was fault-finding. She blamed everybody else. If everybody wasn't so inconsiderate, she wouldn't have this problem. If they didn't ask, she wouldn't have to say yes! It was their fault. . . . Then she came to her senses and to the realization that there was really nobody to blame but herself. She knew why she never said no. And it wasn't very pretty. Somewhere along the line, dutifully accepting assignments and being of genuine service to others had turned into never, ever saying no. If you did, it meant you were a bad person and nobody would like you. The opposite was equally true: if you said yes, it meant you were a good person and everybody would like you.

So Jan learned to say yes. All the time. That way, everybody would like her all the time. Her desire to serve others had been replaced by a desire to be liked by others. Slowly but surely in her bid to win others' acceptance, she found that she had lost her own. To gain it back, she knew exactly what she had to do, and the thought just about killed her.

Two days later the phone rang. "Mom, it's for you!" her daughter yelled from the kitchen. Jan picked up the receiver. It was Selma Wilson. She needed two hundred envelopes stuffed with invitations to the PTA banquet. The little word with the nasty teeth went tearing toward its prey. "Why, y . . . ," Jan began, suddenly pausing to mentally grab the "yes" monster and chain it down. "Selma," Jan began again, hesitantly, "that's an awful lot of envelopes for one person. Have you tried contacting Jim Davis about using the Scout troop? I bet they'd help you as a service project. I appreciate your thinking about me, but I won't be able to give you a hand this time."

The conversation ended. Jan was still breathing. The universe had not ceased to exist. Selma still liked her. As a matter of fact, Selma appreciated her suggestion. But more than anything, when she hung up the phone, Jan liked herself. She liked saying what she meant. Oh, it was frightening. It was awkward. But in spite of the quiver in her voice and the butterflies in her stomach, it was also satisfying. And she didn't have a headache.

There is certainly nothing earth-shattering about coping in this instance. But the accumulation of such small, typical experiences ultimately creates a lasting, enduring sense of self-approval. How did Jan cope?

Jan finally had to stop and ask herself why she was feeling so miserable. That required *introspection*. She had to ask herself, "Why *don't* I just say no?" She had to examine her own thoughts and feelings about the situation. She also had to look at what she was doing and what others were doing. When she did, for just a moment, she began to blame others for her problems. Examining the situation and then determining how she thought and felt about things evidently wasn't enough, because the conclusion she came to was incorrect. She, therefore, had to *reality test* her perceptions. When she did that, she realized that her first reaction was a way of avoiding the fact that it was really her own fault. The resulting *insight* showed her that she failed to say no because she needed to be liked by everybody, so she sacrificed more legitimate needs as well as her own self-respect. She realized, however, that insight was not enough to do anything about her predicament. She had to demonstrate *personal honesty* by accepting responsibility for what she had learned about herself and then choosing to do something about it. To avoid facing what she had learned about herself would be the worst kind of self-deception and personal dishonesty, both of which would only increase her self-disapproval. But, as we saw, Jan chose to continue coping by facing what she feared: saying no. The next time someone asked her to do something she felt she should not accept, she declined. The process of coping (introspection, reality testing, insight, and personal honesty) resulted in Jan's liking herself; something she had not done in a long time. Her ability to deal with the difficulty of saying no was a very self-affirming experience.

Humility

Humility originates in personal strength, not in weakness. Humility is not self-abasement, servile submissiveness, or devaluing ourselves, as so many seem to believe. Rather, it is doing our very best and then quietly leaving our acts, expressions, and accomplishments to speak for themselves. Humility is a strength, a power within those who quietly and unpretentiously have been moved by the Holy Spirit. President Spencer W. Kimball said that "humility is teachableness — an ability to realize that all virtues and abilities are not concentrated in one's self. . . . Humility is gracious, quiet, serene — not pompous, spectacular, nor histrionic. It is subdued, kindly, understanding. . . . It never struts nor swaggers. [Humility is] faithful, quiet works. . . . Humility is repentant. . . . it is the doing of one's best in every case and leaving of one's acts, expressions, and accomplishments to largely speak for themselves" (*The Teachings of Spencer W. Kimball,* ed. Edward L. Kimball [Salt Lake City: Bookcraft, 1982], pp. 232–33).

Humility is the key that unlocks spirituality. Without it, spirituality is virtually impossible. With it, spiritual growth is almost inevitable. Fully understanding our own spiritual nature and being receptive to the promptings of the Lord depend on our knowing what humility is and how to cultivate it in our lives. Without humility, we will never really comprehend our own spiritual nature and capacities. But with humility, we can learn about our own eternal spiritual essence. That is a self-affirming experience of the highest order. The following example illustrates:

" . . . So, Brother Chavez, you see that you couldn't possibly be right."

Hector Chavez looked at the Gospel Doctrine teacher and wasn't sure what to do. Brother Stiles had taken that last quotation completely out of context in an attempt to prove Hector wrong and himself correct, and in the process Brother Stiles had demonstrated all the more his own lack of understanding. Unbeknownst to anyone else, Hector held on his lap the very same book from which the teacher had just read. By reading aloud just one paragraph he could dismantle Brother Stiles' rather weak argument as well as Brother Stiles himself and show the rest of the class members that he was right.

Hector knew he held all the cards. He now had to decide which one of many hands he wanted to play. His first inclination was to make his point and embarrass Brother Stiles in one fell swoop. He thought how easy that would be—and how unhelpful. It would merely be a show, one in which nothing would be taught or learned. In the fraction of the second in which all this thinking transpired, a fleeting image, pale and transparent, appeared before his spiritual eye and then faded away. More than a vague impression but less than a tangible thought, what Hector experienced was an understanding. In a small, mortal, imperfect way, Hector understood the Savior standing in magnificent humility before the Sanhedrin. With legions of angels at his beck and call, with all truth and righteousness at his side, the Savior yet remained silent, uttering only those words necessary to quietly assert his divine heritage. All power was his, and therein lay the complete humility and eloquence of his response to the derisive mockery and abuse. Human weakness responded with divine strength.

Hector sighed. Then he looked at Brother Stiles and smiled warmly. He could see that the entire class was waiting for him to say something. And so he did. "Thank you, Brother Stiles, for responding to my comment. I would very much like to discuss the topic with you in greater detail, but perhaps after class, so as not to take up any more of everyone else's time."

When class was over, Hector met the Gospel Doctrine teacher in the hallway and suggested that they read the quotation in question together. Brother Stiles raised a surprised eyebrow as Hector pulled out his book and invited Brother Stiles to do the same. As they read the quotation in context, it was evident that what Hector had said was correct. Hector gave no reinforcing argument, no chastising remark. He didn't have to say a word. He merely stood there quietly when Brother Stiles cleared his throat and apologized. Brother Stiles then asked Hector to take ten minutes in class next week to explain his thoughts on the subject and correct the teacher's misrepresentation. Hector said he was grateful for the invitation but would let the instructor handle the situation as he saw fit. They shook hands and parted.

Only Hector and Brother Stiles knew of their discussion. If Brother Stiles never mentioned the matter in class again, that would be all right with Hector, too. As he walked home from church that day, he didn't view what had happened as a personal victory. He felt no smugness or pride. More than a vague impression but less than a tangible thought, what Hector experienced was an understanding. In a small, mortal, imperfect way, Hector felt and understood the Savior's love.

This story may seem a fairly obvious example of humility; however, there are subtle points in this story we should look at more closely. For example, had Hector refrained from saying anything to Brother Stiles, that would not have been humility. It might have been fear, inadequacy, perhaps silent anger, but not humility. Humility requires unselfish but responsible behavior. As President Kimball pointed out, humility is courageous. Others might have been intimidated by Brother Stiles. Hector had the necessary humble strength not to be intimidated. He refused to embarrass the teacher and present himself as an authority on the subject being discussed, but he took Brother Stiles aside in private and taught him, quietly, meekly, without retribution or anger. No one else would know from Hector that Hector had been right or that Brother Stiles had been wrong and subsequently corrected. Hector responded to the higher law. His small act of mercy prompted by personal humility resulted in an affirmation of the Savior's love for him, something that couldn't help but affirm his own sense of spiritual goodness and satisfaction.

Avoidance

In virtually all important respects, avoidance is the very opposite of coping. *Fear* is the root of avoidance. Refusing to face personal conflicts we find unpleasant or unsettling leads us to such actions of avoidance as:

Denial: refusing to admit or accept what you know to be true about yourself.

Distortion: changing, twisting, and modifying what you know to be true about yourself in order to deflect the unpleasantness that facing the truth would bring.

Rationalization: excusing yourself from taking responsibility for your actions and their consequences by creating justifications that you know are false and irresponsible.

Avoidance precludes the possibility of personal growth for

two reasons. First, it is an attempt to hide our own imperfections and inadequacies from ourselves. It is a way of pretending that we are better than we believe we are and then accepting those pleasant delusions as our reality. A conflict avoidance approach to living is seductive because it provides immediate relief from the tension of personal trouble spots (underachievement, marital discord, and so forth). But the long-term costs are high. Problems that are not faced and accepted cannot be resolved. Second, denial, distortion, rationalization, and conflict avoidance are all unflattering and inadequate ways of handling personal conflict. They seldom, if ever, improve things. But far more important, if we resort to using these responses too much, we will gradually come to think of ourselves in unflattering and inadequate ways. The adjectives that seem to be consistently associated with avoidance are *weak, cowardly,* and *ineffective.*

The following example shows why so many people come to think of themselves as inadequate because they consistentlty avoid problems they need to face:

"What do you expect me to do, Melissa? Not believe my own child? If he says he didn't do it, he didn't do it!"

Melissa stood there, lips quivering, her arm around her son. His puffy soon-to-be black eye brimming with tears was proof enough of the beating he had just received from someone's hands, but Elaine refused to believe that her son Jared had anything to do with it. As Melissa walked away, saying Jared was not to go near her son David ever again, Elaine took Jared in the house and slammed the door behind her.

"Why don't you play with someone older, Jared?" Elaine asked her son. "Someone who isn't so fragile!" she blurted out.

"But Mom," Jared began, "it's not my fault that . . . "

Before he could finish, Elaine interrupted. "I know, I know. Just don't go down there anymore. All right?"

"Yeah, okay! Can I go play now?" Jared asked.

"Go ahead and play," she said, "and nothing else."

"He's a good boy. He's a good boy. He's a good boy," Elaine thought as she watched Jared leave the house. Like a self-affirming litany of health recited by the terminally ill, Elaine repeated the words over and over again to stave off the sick feeling that grew in her stomach. This wasn't the first time that a mother had come to her door, child in tow, with some sort of complaint. "Your son broke my son's bike! Jared called my daughter a so-and-so! Your son took my son's baseball cards and I want them back now!" Parents, teachers at school and Primary, they all, at one time or another, had called or come by.

Elaine's husband Stan was gone so much that it was usually up to Elaine to handle such things. Lately, she had somehow chosen not to handle things at all. With each new complaint, her need to deny what she knew deep down was true increased. So, it was the other people's fault. Jared's teacher at school was too strict. Primary was too boring. Jared was just misunderstood. With every rationalization, Elaine distanced herself more and more from the true source of the problem: Jared was a troubled little boy. Somehow to Elaine that meant she was a bad mother. By refusing to face the very thing she feared most, she unwittingly made it come true! Elaine's inadequate response to a difficult problem eventually made her feel inadequate, which made her avoid facing the situation all the more. The ensuing vicious circle made her defensive with others and disgusted with herself.

Avoidance comes in as many different forms as there are different people. Each of us avoids issues that are unique to ourselves in unique ways. Yet the common thread throughout is undeniable: refusal to face what we fear or find unpleasant through denial, distortion, rationalization, or conflict avoidance.

63

While Elaine's avoidance included refusing to face her son's difficulty and perhaps her own contribution to the problem, avoidance could be anything from refusing to discuss an important issue with your spouse to refusing to express your opinion in Sunday School. Whenever behavior is motivated out of an unrealistic fear or a need to deny what we know to be true about ourselves, that behavior is avoidance.

Pride

Pride is preoccupation with self. It is self-aggrandizing, self-serving, and self-centered. It is the very opposite of humility, and well it should be, because it comes from an entirely different source. Humility comes from recognizing our dependence and reliance on the Lord for all we are or may ever become. Pride comes from a distorted view of our self-importance, resulting in feelings of superiority, self-sufficiency, accomplishment, and vanity. Pride fails to acknowledge God's hand in all good things, attributing success only to self. More often than not, such tendencies can be nothing more than a way to avoid facing our true, more fundamental feelings of inadequacy and unimportance. Pride is offensive to the Spirit of the Lord. It alienates us from our eternal identity, which makes exercising pride a spiritually self-defeating experience. The following example shows how pride alienates us from our spiritual nature:

Jim loved ward conference. Being the Young Men's President gave him a chance to sit on the stand during priesthood meeting. The seventeen-page report with colored graphs felt substantial in his hands as he leafed through the clean, crisp pages. It would be his turn to speak soon. The talk he had prepared was designed to capture everyone's attention, especially the stake president's.

Jim Braithwaite ran his auxiliary like he ran his business:

efficient, smooth, and with results. He worked hard and liked doing things his way. That's why he rarely delegated, and when he did, it was with express and specific instructions about how something should be done. That way he would be more assured of the outcome. Outcome was what mattered with Jim, no matter the setting: work, home, or church. He based his worth on personal productivity and success. His motto was, "If you want something done right, do it yourself." And so he did. With each success he patted himself, and only himself, on the back. With each rare failure, he'd blame someone else because those were usually the times he'd delegated.

Jim didn't know it, but he was proud. He had no idea that even in the midst of doing work for the kingdom, he was relying solely on the arm of flesh—his own arm. Rather than thanking the Lord for the opportunity to serve and for the talents and abilities he had to use, his offering consisted largely of saying, "Look, see what *I've* done. See what *I've* given you. Surely that makes me a profitable servant."

For Jim the opportunity to serve always turned into an opportunity to impress. Charity became a function of telling people what they needed rather than asking them and then humbly complying. If someone else's suggestion was accepted at the expense of his own, he supported it only halfheartedly. And if things didn't go the way he wanted them to, he felt frustrated and out of control. It was as if he craved chances to speak or be in charge. If he didn't get them, he was sullen and negative. Like so many prideful people, Jim looked to self-aggrandizement as his primary source of reinforcement. And like so many proud people, he was eventually disappointed when that source became bankrupt and empty.

In Jim's case pride showed itself through seemingly righteous acts motivated by unrighteous purposes: using a church calling primarily for self-serving ends. Jim acted out of a need to be recognized as well as a need to succeed in order to feel worthwhile. Real humility, remember, is doing our best and then letting our acts speak for themselves — good works done unobtrusively and without expecting reward. Jim, however, lived for the reward and conducted himself accordingly. In fact, the need for constant external reinforcement is a classic sign of deep feelings of worthlessness. Jim's pride was fueled by the feeling that if he did not produce, if he did not succeed, if he did not get the necessary recognition, he would be left with only what he had inside — a spiritual shallowness that left much to be desired. In short, his pride attempted to deny the very thing it verified: his own spiritual weakness.

It is evident that high levels of spirituality and self-esteem are the result of coping and humility, both attributes that promote a realistic and responsible approach to life's challenges. Moreover, high levels of self-esteem and spirituality are the direct experiencing of our internal/eternal self.

Self-esteem is a manifestation of our capacity to love ourselves and a prerequisite for loving others more fully and unconditionally. Self-esteem is a barometer that tells us, as well as anybody else who cares to look, whether we have a truly durable, internal sense of personal well-being, a well-being that leads to a quiet confidence and self-assuredness. Even though self-esteem is a temporal, psychological concept, it is far from being a trivial spiritual matter, given that the second great commandment instructs us to love our neighbors as we love ourselves.

Enduring self-esteem is not based on social recognition, status, or any other type of achievement. It is a reflection of knowing, trusting, and approving of our own internal psychological character as we have observed it being tested in situations we find difficult. The personal security required to face rather than to avoid difficult problems is the same psychological muscle required to resist the seductive tyranny of pleasing appearances and social approval and, instead, respond to our internal/eternal identity. Self-esteem provides us with the opportunity to experience the self at the highest level of human functioning. Self-esteem makes such experiences self-affirming and personally educational—and that is of paramount importance.

Humility is as essential to developing spirituality as coping is to developing self-esteem. Humility is a quiet strength and a personal resolve to live righteously. It coaxes us to set aside the natural man. It reminds us to remain teachable, and above all, it opens the way to spiritual experiences. Spiritual experiences open the way for us to more fully comprehend the depth and durability of our spiritual capacities. And as we become acquainted with our spiritual capacity, we also learn things about our capacity for eternal goodness that simply cannot be learned in any other way.

Though spirituality and self-esteem are only distant relatives during our mortal experiences, the most essential processes involved in developing personal humility and psychological coping share some rather remarkable similarities.

First, both spirituality and self-esteem require us to be teachable. That is, developing spirituality and developing self-esteem are both growth processes. Self-esteem is the result of learning how to respond to situations that are personally difficult with honesty, integrity, and forthrightness—all qualities that can be as difficult to cultivate as they are rewarding, once they are acquired. Spirituality is the result of learning how to subdue the natural man and yield to the enticements of the Spirit—a task that can also be as difficult as it is rewarding when it is successfully completed. Both learning processes require progressively higher levels of human and spiritual functioning, a task that supplies us with the opportunity to experience and then define ourselves as capable of attaining even higher levels of spiritual and psychological functioning.

Second, both spirituality and self-esteem require acknowledging and overcoming imperfections in the self. Remember, the process of coping is based on the assumption that the self is not perfect and that personal growth can begin when we openly and candidly recognize to ourselves our faults and imperfections. The process of developing spirituality is based on the very similar assumption that we are not perfect and that spiritual growth accompanies a process of continual repentance in which we openly acknowledge to ourselves our faults and imperfections as a first step in striving to overcome them.

Third, spirituality and self-esteem both effect fundamental improvements in our internal sense of personal well-being. The influence of these fundamental internal changes has a ripple effect in other areas of life as well. Self-esteem provides us with realistic confidence and self-assurance that liberate us from unwarranted fear, anxiety, and worry. Self-esteem allows us to more fully express our views and values and eagerly accept and incorporate the favorable and unfavorable consequences of our behavior into an accurate self-image. Spirituality becomes the prime ingredient in and determinant of values, choices, and priorities. It exposes the best of what we are to ourselves and others and, in the process, defines the meaning of life, death, family, and happiness. Spirituality and self-esteem are both powerful internal conditions that organize and influence every other facet of our lives.

These three important similarities between spirituality and self-esteem in turn suggest ways of successfully integrating spirituality and self-esteem in patterns of effective living that have far-reaching implications.

First, our most important point of spiritual or psychological growth is at our own point of greatest weakness and vulnerability. The more fundamental the shortcoming, the more important it is to squarely own up to it. We must honestly and candidly identify and describe our own problems to ourselves in no uncertain terms. Please notice that we are not suggesting that we punish ourselves for having shortcomings. Everybody has shortcomings. Some of us go to greater lengths to hide them than others. But trying to hide them does not alter their existence—it just makes them harder to work with. What we are suggesting is that no problem can be solved before it is identified and openly accepted as a personal or a spiritual shortcoming. It is that simple. If you don't have the courage to own up, you will probably foul up. Pretending just doesn't count in the art of successful living.

Brigham Young clearly understood this basic principle of personal growth and development. He continually urged the Saints to focus their energies on "this one thing, the sanctification of our own hearts, the purifying of our own affections, the preparing of ourselves for the approach of the events that are hastening upon us" (in *Journal of Discourses,* 9:3). Growth is a process that starts when we willingly face our most fundamental internal motives and desires. That can only be done by stripping away our false fronts and pretenses and probing deeply within ourselves. The following illustration clarifies this difficult but essential step in our own spiritual and psychological growth:

Phil's hand trembled as he looked at his bleeding knuckles and then at the fist-sized hole, jagged and sharp in the otherwise smooth surface of the wall. No one spoke. No one moved. Lisa, the thirteen-year-old, quietly whimpered. The other children had long since been banished to their rooms upstairs, where they could hear only muffled explosions of the violent clash of tempers erupting below them.

The pale wash of the television screen cast its flickering shadows over the room where they stood frozen in their places, immobilized by a loss of what to do now, what to do about it later. The dull ache in Phil's hand slowly crawled to his head. Where searing rage and anger had dominated, now only a numbing emptiness remained. Addie, his wife, took a wad of well-used tissue from her pocket and wiped the tears from her eyes. She then bent down to pick up the pieces of the dish she had thrown at Phil, wishing there was some way to pick up the pieces of a nearly shattered marriage.

Still no one spoke. No one looked at anyone else. The barrage and counterbarrage of verbal abuse and senseless violence left them enervated and spent. Suddenly, Phil's big frame shook with a heavy sigh. Mumbling something that resembled an awkward apology and justification rolled into one, he ran out the door, leaving it ajar. As if on cue, Lisa ran to Addie, throwing her arms around her mother in an attempt to console as well as seek consolation. All Addie could think about was how they would explain the hole in the wall when the home teachers came tomorrow evening.

Breakfast. Cold cereal for the kids, eggs for Dad. Lunches being made, teeth being brushed, hair being combed. The following morning was just like any other. Business as usual in a home where a hurricane had raged the night before. Each one, from eldest to youngest, pushed from their minds the images of last night's stormy turbulence. The sickness of the altercation wasn't restricted simply to the violent behavior itself. It was all too evident in their silence as well. Their silence was intended to protect the family, but it could ultimately destroy it instead, because silence masked the deadliness of their self-inflicted wound from themselves as much as from others.

The home teachers came, the stories were told, and the wrecked wall humorously dismissed along with inquiries into the family's welfare. Facades were maintained in Relief Society and elders quorum, appearances of strength covered up weakness, and illusions of family unity smoothed the surface of deep chaos. The desire to wear the aspect of a good, happy family kept them from being one. As long as they simply covered up their most serious problem by attempting to prove to others and themselves that nothing was wrong, nothing could ever really be right. Their greatest opportunity for achieving spiritual and emotional well-being had to come through facing their greatest spiritual and emotional difficulty. All efforts short of that paled in hopeless comparison.

The second major step in both spiritual and psychological growth usually requires us to resolve our most blatant spiritual or psychological shortcomings and vulnerabilities. This point is extremely important. It tells us where to invest our time and energy in personal improvement. The more serious the psychological or spiritual problem, the more important it is to deal with it *now*. That's right, right *now*. No pretending, and no substitutes. Fixing a leaky faucet won't make the car run better. Experience has taught us that this step can be very difficult. People usually like to work their way up to the big things. You know, sort of a warm-up that's not too scary. Sorry! That's called rationalization. In our view, you face the worst first, because as soon as the most difficult issue has been faced, or discussed, or identified, everybody relaxes a little. Rapport is easier, tension starts to dissipate, and people start problem-solving more productively. Why? Because the worst is over. There is nothing more to be afraid of. The hardest part is over. But before that happens, most people are uncomfortable waiting for the dreaded event to happen, whether it's confusion, confrontation, or simply a clear definition of the problem. The continuation of our example illustrates the importance of taking on the most difficult problems first.

A present! He always got her a present as a peace offering of sorts. It was his attempt to soothe the hurt without ever really dealing with it: emotional damage awarded emotionless damages. He would also attend to the smaller infractions he knew he was guilty of: help more around the house, spend more time with the kids, or share some nights out with Addie. He'd work even harder, make bigger sales with bigger commissions, fix the house up, and spend more on vacations. She would be a better wife, prepare dinner on time, iron his shirts, and clean the house more often. She would be more attentive to his needs, keeping herself in better shape.

Round and round they both went, focusing on every little problem in hopes that somehow the big problem would go away—efforts otherwise commendable but in this case worse than useless. They engaged in the nonessentials to avoid facing the absolute essential. From their parents' example, the children learned that unbridled anger was not unbridled at all. It was acceptable behavior. It was excusable and easily dismissed. Nevertheless, the thirteen-year-old was doing inexplicably worse in school, the nine-year-old's nightmares were more frequent and intense, and the six-year-old struck out at his friends for little, if any, reason.

At first it was easy for Addie to remain oblivious to the troubling signs of her troubled children. But gradually, as it became more evident, as friends and neighbors carefully but undeniably hinted at this or that child's behavior, it seemed at every turn there was a nagging reminder that her family was different—different, and not well. So she read books, books on marriage, books on families, books on being a better parent. With each book she read, she effectively distanced herself from really facing the problem that counted most, the problem that no book could resolve.

So it happened again. And again. And again. Until one morning she couldn't quite cover the emotional scars with a stiff upper lip and firm resolve. Looking in the mirror, she didn't recognize the woman staring blankly back at her. She looked too old, too tired, too crestfallen to be someone she knew. Then in a rush of overwhelming anger, frustration, and sorrow, she bowed her head and sobbed uncontrollably. Oppressive doom and sheer hopelessness enwrapped her like a dark shroud. Staccato-sharp images of her life with Phil punctuated the anguish of the present and the memories of the past: a temple marriage with covenants made but now broken, children born in hope but now raised in fear, life once bright with limitless dreams but now tarnished with debilitating reality. Where things mattered the most, they had succeeded the least. As the vision cracked, crumbled, and fell apart right before her eyes, "We have failed," was all she could utter.

As a result of facing problems we usually avoid, we start to affirm and improve ourselves. This gradual growth eventually allows us to accomplish what was originally inconceivable. There is an interesting paradox in this step. Facing up to both spiritual and psychological shortcomings involves immediate discomfort. That involves candidly recognizing that we are less than we might hope for, which is always an unsettling experience. But ironically, clearly labeling and understanding our personal imperfections is precisely what arouses in us the motivation to change them. Internal discomfort as a source of motivation for personal growth is not something to be short-circuited. It is normal, natural, and inevitable in healthy individuals. You see, increasing our capacity to tolerate the self-imposed discomfort associated with facing personal imperfections with candor and honesty is personal growth and development. The very act of facing what we tend to avoid is how we acquire confidence and belief in ourselves. And with every attempt to face forthrightly what we are displeased with in ourselves, we add to our own internal capacity for effective problem solving. Spiritual and psychological growth is a process, a style of traveling, not a destination. This important point is illustrated in the following:

That night, when Phil went to bed, he found a rectangular piece of paper lying on his pillow. As his eyes adjusted to the darkness, it became all too clear that he was looking at his and Addie's temple marriage certificate. He asked Addie what was going on. All she said was, "We've failed, Phil." He wanted to scoff, object, derisively demand an explanation. Instead, the ensuing silence was evidence enough that Phil understood what Addie meant. Even in his most lucid moments he refused to imagine that his marriage was actually in jeopardy. As topsy-turvy as things had gotten, the last thing he wanted was to lose his wife. And now his greatest fear was coming true. Phil sat down on the edge of the bed. With head in hands he whispered, "What have I done? What have I done?" The sheer tragedy of their predicament no longer afforded any alternative other than to pierce the repugnant, festering core of their diseased marriage.

Addie shook her head and said that he was not the only one to blame. Somewhere, somehow, in the fifteen years of their life together, they had both learned to accept and foster the destructive behavior that infected their marriage. Sitting in the darkness, they both knew with excruciating clarity, beyond doubt or question, the gravity of their situation. They knew what they were, what they had become. They'd read about, heard about, even known couples who hurled objects, obscenities, and abhorrence at each other. To place themselves in that category seemed inconceivable. Yet they had to. Someone had to come out and say it. Knowing it or thinking it wasn't enough. They had to share the words that would once and for all shed the light on the darkest corner of their lives. Moments passed in silence until Addie spoke the unspeakable. "We are a violent, abusive couple. We have injured ourselves and our children. We are sick and we need help."

Like the sweeping beacon of a lighthouse, her words clearly, undeniably, opened a lighted path through the once impenetrable darkness. Their ensuing conversation was awkward and difficult, yet because the worst had been said, the most feared had been faced, they were able to do what they had never been able to do before: candidly share their innermost thoughts and feelings, hopes and fears—especially their fears.

As the night wore on, Phil reveled in the closeness he felt toward Addie. Somehow, opening up to her, letting her in where long ago he had shut her out, seemed gratifying and right. They both marveled that this newfound sense of intimacy and sharing would come on the heels of such dire circumstances. They were puzzled that this closeness came only after they fell to the very bottom of their own personal pit. All their previous attempts to skirt around the gaping abyss had merely brought them added sorrow. Only when they leaped headlong into the gaping darkness could they begin to see the light. Yet even now, as they looked upward, they knew there was still the grueling climb ahead.

Morning came all too soon. Neither of them slept, really. They both just lay there, lost in reflections of what had transpired and of what was yet to come. As Phil shaved and Addie put on her makeup, neither spoke, as if words would break the fragile spell of intimacy that their talking had cast the night before. Phil's hand trembled, causing him to nick the corner of his chin. Wincing, he let the razor fall from his hand as he pressed a finger to the cut. He then leaned both hands against the sink and let his head drop to his chest.

Addie stopped, mascara in hand, and asked him what was wrong. "I'm afraid," he whispered. "Of what?" she asked, already knowing what he was going to say. Phil recounted his feelings of last night, of the sweetness that accompanied their candor and honesty. He then told her that he feared losing the peace and contentment that facing the worst together had brought them. He told her how afraid he was that they might not ever be able to retrieve that intimacy and peacefulness again. Addie wanted to respond with assurances to the contrary, but she knew they were false. She too was afraid that their newfound hope would soon wane.

In a desperate need to hold on to what was left of the night before, they agreed to set aside time to talk about those things that were once hushed up and ignored. The prospect of opening doors they had always kept closed, entering places they had never been, was both frightening and exhilarating.

They decided to take turns. They alternated determining what the topic of discussion would be from session to session. The only requirement was that they had to remain as honest as they were the night they stopped covering up and started owning up. As the weeks went by, they noticed that the honesty, the opening up, caused the most discomfort as well as the most satisfaction in their discussions. It was as if by recognizing and admitting to the worst things about themselves that they recognized their own ability to deal with them. They could never have known that they had the strength to overcome their greatest problems until they actually tried. Their best discussions, the ones that brought the most satisfaction and results, were also the ones where they dealt with the heaviest issues. They knew that if it was difficult to say, it was worth saying.

Every once in awhile Addie would mentally pull away while Phil was speaking. She sat and looked at the man in front of her. Inside she smiled. It was a smile of promise and assurance. This was the Phil she had married fifteen years ago: honest, open, trying to listen in order to understand. Her love and respect grew with Phil's increased willingness to recognize and confront his weaknesses. Addie couldn't understand why so many men felt they had to hide their fears and weaknesses in order to be admired or respected, when as far as she was concerned, the exact opposite was true.

Phil and Addie still had their ups and down, that was for sure, but as the weeks and months went by, a change was taking place, gradual, imperceptible day by day, but a change none-theless. It manifested itself mostly in the comfortableness of the relationship. There was a casual ease between the two that had never existed before. Addie and Phil accepted one another on the basis of what they really were—their weaknesses as well as their strengths. And the more they were able to deal with their weaknesses, the more approving and accepting they became of themselves and each other. They knew they could never let down. Times were the roughest when they became closed and avoidant. They understood that their relationship as well as their personal spiritual and emotional well-being required a continuing process of honesty and forthrightness in facing and then overcoming what they feared the most. A complete resolution of Phil and Addie's problems will require both spiritual and psychological attention.

Remember, spirituality and self-esteem are the two sides of the same human coin. One influences spiritual development; the other, psychological development. But they are both, in their purest forms, a reflection and a result of our internal/eternal self in the process of becoming perfected. Both of these prized attributes grow best in soil that is rich with honesty, integrity, and willingness to face the imperfections that are inherent in our mortal existence.

Even though spirituality and self-esteem represent two do-mains of our mortal experience, their growth and development share many similarities. Coping and humility, the most essential ingredients in self-affirming experiences, are similar indeed. They are both manifestations of inner strength, quiet accomplishment, and enduring teachableness. Avoidance and pride, on the other hand, are the staple ingredients in self-defeating experiences. Not surprisingly, they also share a number of significant similarities. They represent the lower levels of human functioning, such as immediate gratification, escape from fear, responsibility, and conflict, and an exaggerated and unrealistic sense of self-importance.

Not surprisingly, it is difficult, if not completely impossible, to reach our psychological and spiritual capacities when we function at the lower levels of human effectiveness. Both spirituality and self-esteem, though separate in most respects, require the highest levels of human functioning. What we learn to think of ourselves and how we actually behave, both spiritually and psychologically, depends in large measure on the experiences we create for ourselves by being consistently humble or proud, coping or avoidant.

Chapter Six

Cultivating Self-Esteem

Now comes the hard part! It's time to shift our focus from theory to application. That is not an easy task. There simply are no universal recipes equally applicable to all situations and individuals. Fortunately, however, there are general principles, which can prove useful to those of us who are searching for higher self-esteem, regardless of differences in our individual personalities or circumstances. When they are properly understood, these principles can be applied very successfully to individual problems. But make no mistake about it. Successfully applying these principles in our individual lives is impossible without our first understanding them.

We will approach that difficult task in three steps. First, we will review some important principles about self-esteem and the role coping plays in its development. Second, we will discuss several common and unfortunate myths about self-esteem. Our intent is to expose the absurdity of these views in hopes of dispelling their misleading appeal. Third, because we consider it extremely important to recognize and acknowledge the styles of avoidance that deter us from cultivating our self-esteem, we will describe several basic styles of avoidance and their coping counterparts. Then we will conclude with a brief example of one person's avoidant style and his eventual ability to replace it with coping responses, which enhance self-esteem.

Basic Principles of Self-Esteem

Principle 1

Self-esteem is the result of our consistently avoiding or coping with problem situations we find unpleasant or uncomfortable.

Our individual response styles are varying mixtures of coping and avoidance. Some of us are terribly bothered by things that others hardly even notice. We all have problems that concern us, and to the degree that our individual response style favors coping over avoidance, we can expect gradual increases in self-esteem over time. The converse is equally true. To the degree that our individual response style favors avoidance over coping, we can expect gradual decreases in our personal self-esteem over time.

High or low levels of self-esteem are not the result of dramatic events, significant gains or losses of status and position, or social popularity or acceptance. Self-esteem is based on something far more fundamental. The moment-by-moment events in our lives furnish the material from which we construct our own self-evaluations. Self-esteem is, ultimately, a reflection of the kind of person we perceive ourselves to be when we avoid or cope with the problems of life that surround us. When we face, understand, and resolve problems, our self-confidence, personal approval, and personal security increase. Patterns of excessive avoidance, however, breed just the opposite reaction. The very act of avoidance, by denying, distorting, and psychologically evading, precludes feelings of personal adequacy because of the inherent inadequacy of these responses.

Principle 2

Self-evaluative thoughts and feelings are a psychological reality for most of us.

Most people regularly notice what they do, how they feel, and how they feel about what they do. People regularly engage in a process of noticing, monitoring, thinking about, and evaluating their own behavior and beliefs. It would be unfortunate and short-sighted to consider personal awareness as nothing more than thoughts and observations about ourselves, however. It is far more than that. Virtually all human experiences have emotions associated with them. Some emotions can be more intense and compelling than others, but that is a variation in degree.

Self-evaluative feelings can be extremely intense, particularly when we observe our own tendencies to cope with or to avoid conflicts. A high-quality coping response in the face of conflict can easily create intense feelings of self-approval, confidence, and personal satisfaction. Coping is a self-affirming experience because it allows us to experience the self as strong, capable, and forthright. Self-affirming experiences are the result of the psychological behavior inherent in the process of coping itself. We know of numerous individuals who were well pleased with themselves even though the conflict they confronted remained unresolved. This pleasant and sometimes intense experience is the inevitable consequence of the satisfying behaviors inherent in coping. No matter how strategic a retreat from conflict may appear, retreating still invokes a reflexive negative self-evaluation.

Self-evaluation goes on for virtually all of us almost all the time. Sometimes it takes place at higher levels of clarity and explicitness than others, but the results usually remain the same. Self-evaluative thoughts and feelings express what we intellectually see and emotionally experience about ourselves when our fundamental character is revealed in anxiety-arousing situations.

Principle 3

Paradoxically, any attempt we make to clearly identify our own patterns of avoidance is a coping response.

Coping requires a realistic self-examination and a willingness to face unpleasant realities about ourselves that we usually avoid. All of that requires us to function at higher levels of risk and personal responsibility than we are generally accustomed to. Although such an experience can be uncomfortable, it produces growth. You see, personal growth is anchored to an increasing understanding of ourselves and the world we live in and to increasingly effective problem-solving. Personal growth requires each of us to identify and label imperfections in the self as the first step in improving the self. Identifying and labeling imperfections can feel uncomfortable and threatening. But that is the beginning of the very coping process that allows growth and positive change to take place.

Common Myths about Self-Esteem

Let us now take a look both at the myths that tend to overshadow the principles of self-esteem we have just examined and at the realities that dispel those myths.

The Myth of Unconditional Love

Many of us erroneously believe that if we are the recipients of constant doses of unconditional love, self-esteem is sure to follow. The "bucket of love" metaphor is overused: "If your bucket of love is full, you'll feel good about yourself and others." This rationale leads us to think that if disappointments are minimized, rejection is avoided, and our abilities are never questioned (that is, we are accepted unconditionally and unceasingly), our self-esteem will remain unquestioned and intact. Many unwary individuals fall prey to the false idea that others can and should act as a constant source of their well-being. In other words, according to this myth, if we suffer from low self-esteem, the reason is that those around us are not loving us enough. It is their fault and has nothing to do with us.

Reality

We assert that although others do contribute to how we feel about ourselves, if our family, our friends, and our associates spent all their time being nonjudgmental and uncritical and if they deflected every potential scrape and bump coming our way, they would actually be depriving us of the very experiences that provide important problem-solving opportunities and the chance to develop the internal self, which builds self-esteem.

This myth can be placed in proper perspective when we remind ourselves that the purpose of our earthly existence is to be separated from the Father and his protection so that in the face of mortal trials we can grow.

The Bucket of Love Myth, Part 2

A fascinating corollary to the myth of unconditional love, or the "bucket of love" concept, implies that if you're feeling down, if your self-esteem is low, if your bucket of love is nearly empty, then do something for yourself: get a new hairdo, go to the movies, buy some new clothes, or even just brush your teeth. The theory behind this myth is that if you focus solely on yourself when you lack self-esteem, that will lift your spirits and give you a moment's respite that will renew and rejuvenate you. Your bucket of love will be refilled and, in turn, you will be able to fill others' buckets.

Reality

We do agree that we all need to pamper ourselves occasionally, but escape should not be the primary means of combating low self-esteem. Escape merely delays the moment when the real issues, the real causes of inadequate self-esteem, must be confronted. Escape is actually avoidance, which temporarily assuages personal hurts but at the expense of facing and ridding ourselves of the true source of the pain.

The Myth That Success Produces Self-Esteem

The pernicious myth that success produces self-esteem is encouraged by well-intended but misguided parents who assume that their children's self-esteem can be nurtured through multitudinous opportunities to perform and compete: dance, piano, clogging, football, basketball, soccer, and so forth. The list is long, but the intention is as short as it is short-sighted. With such opportunities comes the opportunity to win, to succeed, to be better than peers. The myth that success produces self-esteem requires that we must win to feel good about ourselves. Self-esteem is seen as being something in short supply and is therefore reserved only for the victorious. In contrast, low self-esteem is bounteously served in its abundance to the lesser but infinitely more numerous failures or merely average people of the world.

Casualties of this myth show up as massive, self-debilitating chunks in adulthood. Happiness and self-worth are restricted to those who win and succeed. At home their kids are the cutest and brightest; at work they make the most money or have the biggest offices; at church they hold more prestigious positions.

Reality

We can all see the folly of this myth. It focuses entirely upon outcome and ignores the process through which self-esteem is achieved. Self-esteem is thought to be a by-product of winning or achieving some goal in a competitive process that renders trust, honest effort, integrity, and cooperation irrelevant. Although it is true that success can bring a sense of accomplishment, which is both reinforcing and reaffirming, success is neither necessary nor sufficient to produce lasting self-esteem (consider, for example, Marilyn Monroe, Judy Garland, Howard Hughes, and Ernest Hemingway).

We maintain that the essential element in building self-esteem is the process — the process of coping, or choosing to face difficult challenges regardless of the outcome. When effort and commitment to the activity are the focus, the process itself becomes the source of self-satisfaction and self-approval. We do not depend on external judges declaring us the winner and therefore worthy of feeling good about ourselves. In the words of T. S. Eliot, "For us, there is only the trying. The rest is not our business" (*East Coker,* in *The Four Quartets,* New York: Harcourt, Brace, and Co., 1943). The Savior is the perfect exemplar of this concept of process. He returned to his own Nazareth to bring his gospel to those he knew as a youth, yet they scorned him. They even attempted to stone and kill him. Was he a success? Did he win many disciples? Did the outcome matter? Did it preclude him from trying?

The Success Produces Self-Esteem Myth, Part 2

The myth that productivity equals self-esteem is an interesting corollary of the myth that success produces self-esteem. The idea here is if you get a lot done, if you work hard, you will really feel good about yourself, and your self-esteem will soar. This myth has brought about a boom in the schedule book business. The more organized, deliberate, and busy you are, the happier you'll be. Each task that you can check off as having been done is one more notch on your self-esteem six-shooter.

Reality

The reality is that people tend to feel like massive failures if they don't get everything done, and they feel very pressured to get everything done. Furthermore, some of the most miserable people we encounter are those who are compulsively driven to accomplish more and more. Yet, even when they do accomplish even more, it never seems to be enough. It appears that external achievements seldom truly satisfy internal deficits.

The Myth That Popularity Produces Self-Esteem

At one time or another, didn't we all think that if we could be a cheerleader, captain of the football team, or run around with the popular crowd, that we would feel much better about ourselves? Probably every adolescent has. The problem is that an abundance of adults are still thinking like teenagers. They believe that if they can be liked by all, they can remain invulnerable to social criticism — a sure downer on the self-esteem scale. So, instead of trying out for cheerleader, they bake loaves of bread or batches of cookies for the neighborhood in hopes of being liked by everybody. Instead of going out for the football team, they try out for office clown, cracking jokes and back-slapping in an equal bid for popularity and acceptance. And nothing has really changed since adolescence as far as running around with the popular crowd is concerned. We see a proliferation of country clubs and various other social groups and people clamoring to be admitted to them.

Reality

The search for social acceptance and invulnerability to rejection is a sure-fire formula for self-esteem: *low* self-esteem. If we use that type of impression management, the only result will be that our sense of self-worth decreases. For even if acceptance is achieved, it is acceptance of the facade, the phony self. That inevitably leaves us thinking, "They wouldn't accept me if they really knew what I was like." Certainly that is a far cry from genuine self-esteem.

The Myth of Following the Leader to Self-Esteem

Although not unlike the popularity myth, the myth of following the leader to self-esteem has a subtle difference that warrants examination. The key word of this myth is *compliance,* unhealthy compliance. This myth also has its origins in childhood. Many of us were taught that we should unquestioningly obey those in authority over us: parents, schoolteachers, and adults in general. The rationale was that we would be happier by listening to and complying with those "who knew better." By being "seen and not heard," we would feel good about ourselves because we were doing the right thing.

Reality

Childhood does require sufficient boundaries as well as obedience to those responsible for guiding us, but when the attitude of unquestioning obedience continues into adulthood, self-esteem is not likely to result. First of all, self-esteem requires self-directedness. If we are willing to follow others blindly, and we abdicate our own role in considering the consequences of our behavior, we deny the very essence of self-esteem, which is volitional decision-making and personal responsibility. Self-esteem flourishes with such statements as, "I choose to do this and will take responsibility for the outcome, not so much because so-and-so told me to do it, but because I choose to do it." If our sense of worth is wrapped up in blindly following authority figures or if we leech our identity and direction from them, then, in the absence of authority figures and lacking a true identity of our own, we are left confused, vulnerable, and devoid of self-esteem.

This overview is by no means an exhaustive look at the myriad myths and misunderstandings about self-esteem. You very likely have heard of others or may even harbor some of your own. If you ever catch yourself thinking, "I'll feel better about myself once I get this, or buy that, or once so-and-so likes me, or when I become this or achieve that," and if the outcome is your only concern, chances are you're living to some degree or another at least one myth of self-esteem.

Enhancing Self-Esteem

There is no magic, no secret formula, no innovative technique that will guarantee high self-esteem. We must instead be willing to take a hard, long, honest look at ourselves and face the things we tend to avoid.

Coping is the opposite of avoidance. Instead of resulting in guilt, personal stagnation, loss of productivity, and lack of self-esteem as avoiding conflict does, coping with conflict results in confidence, personal understanding, greater productivity, and increased self-esteem. Coping is a growth-oriented process in which personal development is the inevitable result of facing, understanding, and resolving conflict. Coping is also a process that involves psychological ingredients fundamentally different from those involved in avoidance. The two most important components of coping are psychological risk-taking and personal responsibility.

Psychological Risk-Taking

Psychological risk-taking is necessary if we are to cope with conflict, because when we move nearer to facing unpleasant impulses, emotions, motives, and experiences, we risk possible injury to our reputation, loss of self-esteem, disapproval of others, and personal discomfort. We must be willing to face those psychological risks before we can resolve underlying conflicts. The risks we must face seem to fall into two categories: internal risk and interpersonal risk.

Internal risk: results from increased awareness of unacceptable or feared characteristics within ourselves. Internal risk follows such processes as introspection, letting down defenses, or attempting personal challenges. It is the risk of knowing — the risk of finding out about ourselves, of facing the possibility that our greatest fears are in fact true. For example, introspection may lead us to discover strong resentment for a family member, or letting down our defenses may reveal an embarrassing fear, or attempting a challenge may uncover our inability to perform.

Interpersonal risk: results from allowing others to see us as we really are. Interpersonal risk follows such events as confrontations, personal disclosures, or social participation. It is the risk of being known — the risk of letting others know who we really are and thus risking their disapproval, rejection, or criticism. For example, disclosing our commitment to a particular belief may lead to rejection by a friend who rejects the belief, or participation in a group project may lead others to discover and criticize our inabilities.

Sometimes, both internal and interpersonal risks are involved in a single event. For example, our confronting a colleague about why he or she seems to avoid us may result in our being told that we talk too much. That confrontation involves an internal fear of discovering a personal problem as well as an interpersonal fear of being criticized or rejected.

Personal Responsibility

Personal responsibility is a willingness to see ourselves as causal agents — or at least contributors — to the outcome of our lives. It is accepting responsibility for what happens to us as a result of the decisions we make, the actions we take, and the attitudes we maintain. Personally responsible individuals realize that although they cannot influence some factors in their lives (the weather, accidents, the actions of others), they can control the course of their own personal development. Rather than forfeit control over their lives to fate or circumstance, they strive to increase their control over themselves. Rather than complain about their problems, they realize that if they are the cause, they can also be the cure. They understand the law of the harvest at a personal level and recognize the truth of the scripture, "all men shall reap a reward of their works" (Alma 9:28). They consciously work to narrow the gap between things as they would like them to be and things as they presently are.

Personally responsible people also have a special type of insight: they have a high degree of self-perception and are able to make the connections between what they see inside themselves and what they see outside. For example, responsible people might recognize that their insecurity about expressing themselves causes them to avoid especially articulate people. They would also realize that to feel more comfortable around their articulate associates, they need either to become more articulate themselves or become comfortable with their present speaking abilities. When they act on their recognition, they are coping with personal conflict.

Being able to recognize and understand our own style of avoiding difficult and uncomfortable things about ourselves is a critical step in enhancing self-esteem. We need to keep three observations about avoidance clearly in mind:

1. Psychological avoidance in all of its infinite varieties and subtle manifestations is the essence of ineffective behavior.

2. Our actions of avoidance are always motivated by a desire to escape from the fear or the anxiety associated with events we may find unpleasant or frightening. Psychological avoidance is not specific behaviors. It is what motivates the behavior. The quintessential quality of avoidant behavior is the attempt to escape from conflict and the discomfort associated with it. To truly understand our own avoidant behavior, then, we must

understand the function any behavior serves for us at the time we use that behavior.

3. The concept of avoidance has a spiritual dimension. In fact, that dimension may well prove to be the most important consideration of all. A careful reading of Moses 4 suggests that Satan himself was intimately associated with the first appearance of avoidant behavior in the world. Adam and Eve partook of the forbidden fruit in the Garden of Eden at the specific request and deceptive encouragement of Satan. The result, as we all know, was that Adam and Eve learned to know both good and evil.

Immediately after they partook of the fruit, Adam and Eve heard the voice of the Lord, and their reflexive response was to hide themselves. In other words, once Adam and Eve knew good from evil as a result of yielding to Satan's enticement to partake of the forbidden fruit, their instinctive response was to *avoid* the Lord rather than own up to their wrongdoing:

"And they heard the voice of the Lord God, as they were walking in the garden, in the cool of the day; and Adam and his wife went to hide themselves from the presence of the Lord God amongst the trees of the garden.

"And I, the Lord God, called unto Adam, and said unto him: Where goest thou?

"And he said: I heard thy voice in the garden, and I was afraid, because I beheld that I was naked, and I hid myself.

"And I, the Lord God, said unto Adam: Who told thee thou wast naked? Hast thou eaten of the tree whereof I commanded thee that thou shouldst not eat?" (Moses 4:15–17).

The theological importance of these verses goes far beyond the idea of psychological avoidance, of course. But they do rather pointedly suggest several things:

1. After Adam and Eve lost their innocence in the Garden of Eden and understood both good and evil, they also acquired

the capacity to feel ashamed and self-conscious about their own behavior.

2. When Adam and Eve first acted in ways they were ashamed of, they had a reflexive tendency to hide themselves from the Lord.

3. The tendency to avoid (hide) behavior individuals are personally ashamed of is probably not limited to religious events.

4. The inclination to hide from the consequences of undesirable behavior first appeared after Adam and Eve's first exchange with Satan, at which time they did something that had been forbidden by the Lord.

5. In the absence of a Savior and repentance, spiritual growth would have been impossible and the future development of humankind would have been fundamentally compromised.

This spiritual account of avoidance and its consequences parallels our secular understanding of personal growth and development in some rather startling ways. We have already suggested that avoidance is an unsatisfying psychological response for most of us in most situations. We have also suggested that when we behave in unflattering ways, we have an almost reflexive tendency to hide those unpleasant realities from ourselves and others. That process of hiding significantly retards our personal growth and development.

The conclusion is rather obvious. Personal repentance, or a process very similar to it, is as essential to psychological growth as it is to spiritual development. Repentance and coping both involve recognizing and owning up to our own shortcomings, accepting (rather than hiding from) those unpleasant realities, and then using the internal emotional discomfort caused by our self-perceptions as our motivation to strive for self-improvement.

Styles of Psychological Avoidance and Their Coping Alternatives

Impression Management

Impression Management is attempting to make yourself more appealing and acceptable to others by pretending to be what you believe others would like you to be. Mild forms of Impression Management are commonly seen in the early phases of dating. More severe forms are seen in adults who conform to standards, values, and expectations to the point they actually sacrifice their identity in trying to fit in.

This style of avoidance allows people to hide behind an appealing interpersonal facade and minimize the risk of being known or rejected by others. Approval is gained by complying with the expectations of others. Impression Management often becomes a style of life in which individuals constantly try to gain approval by satisfying others' needs and expectations in almost all situations. Psychologically, Impression Management is an extremely dangerous form of conflict avoidance because it denies individuals the opportunity to cultivate their own unique individuality and God-given talents. Furthermore, it also seems to create extremely harsh self-evaluative feelings because the individuals experience their own inadequacy and weakness so clearly and explicitly when they beg for the approval of others by conforming to their expectations. All of that maneuvering is to avoid truly knowing themselves or being intimately known by others.

A Coping Alternative

A coping response to replace Impression Management requires understanding that the more you are yourself, the more you give people an opportunity to like what you really are. The unavoidable flip side is that being yourself also provides others the opportunity not to like you. Most impression managers will say that if they acted as they really are, no one would like them. Our experience has been that these folks have been faking it for so long they really don't know what the outcome would be if they let down the facades. We recommend that they try being themselves (expressing their opinion, dressing the way they want to, sending back the too-done steak) in a situation where they typically want to manage impressions. Many of our clients have reported that the resultant self-approval far outweighs any perceived fear of rejection. Furthermore, they find that others actually appreciate them for their willingness to be genuine! Who wants to be friends with a phony, anyway?

Help Me Find the Way

As a style of avoidance, Help Me Find the Way is acting as if you understand or know far less than you actually do, while treating others as if they know far more. Here is a typical example of this fascinating and disarming style of avoidance:

You are talking with an acquaintance who asks a question that calls upon your professional expertise. You feel uncomfortable having to respond directly, so you hedge with such statements as, "It could be" or "I'm not sure, but" and so on.

You belittle yourself because you fear you may put her off with what you know. So you play dumb. Before she can ask you another question, you ask her one, even though you already know the answer and it's evident she doesn't. In your seemingly innocent, ignorant way (two excellent examples are "Gee, I'm just a down-home, country bumpkin — yup, yup" and the "Gosh, I'm so scatterbrained; could you help me find my head, please?"), you begin to answer the question you asked, all the while making it sound as if it's your friend who is coming up with the answer! You do that by giving the answers prefaced with such questions as, "Do you think it could be ... ?" or "What do you think about ... ?" When your acquaintance does respond, you quickly rephrase what she says, adding a little bit more of your own answer, and then you thank her for being so perceptive and smart. Your friend is very flattered because you make her feel as if you are learning so much from her.

The essence of the Help Me Find the Way routine, then, is to play dumb in a very inquisitive way to avoid both conflict and responsibility for simple self-declarations and other forms of psychological initiatives in problem-solving. Used skillfully, this routine allows individuals who use it to comfortably hide behind a shield of flattery and perceived eagerness to learn. They are seldom required to face difficult issues squarely because they understand the issues so much less perfectly than you do. Furthermore, because of the barrage of questions they so adeptly ask, they never really say what they think and feel beyond what they want you to know, which is usually superficial and innocuous. Their style allows them to function at very low levels of personal risk and responsibility.

A Coping Alternative

Although the coping alternative to Help Me Find the Way is a bit more difficult than the coping alternative for Impression Management, it requires the same basic ingredient: you must be willing to be honest with yourself and others. Such honesty requires risk and responsibility. Rather than avoiding being known by others, you express your thoughts and feelings openly. As with Impression Management, you run the risk of being accepted or rejected. Either outcome requires the responsibility of taking ownership of the causes and consequences of your behavior. In doing so, you no longer manipulate others in a self-effacing way. Instead, you treat yourself and others with respect. Both risk-taking and being responsible are coping mechanisms that have inherently strong self-approving responses. With increased self-approval comes increased self-esteem.

Walt Disney Productions

Users of the Walt Disney Productions style of avoidance find something good in almost any situation, no matter how bad it really is. People who use this style of avoidance tend to be patient, long-suffering, and unrealistically optimistic. They almost always see the good in others and almost never respond to the bad. They often receive many kind words and compliments; however, closer examination shows a marked difference between individuals who are truly "the salt of the earth" and the ones we are describing here. The telltale signs of real Walt Disney Productions people look like this:

They avoid conversations about the cocaine problem, world hunger, economic problems of the elderly, and growing concerns about such social problems as child abuse, crime, divorce, and violence.

They never discuss family problems or conflicts. If you are so insensitive as even to try (how could you!), they will break down in tears or give some quick, pat answer to dismiss your concern that your sister Shirley is crazy (wearing a pith helmet and lederhosen to her bank teller job is just a phase!).

They never criticize a waiter, auto mechanic, cab driver, or plumber. If they don't see a problem in the first place, how can they criticize the person that supposedly caused it? So what if you ordered chicken and got a liverwurst sandwich. Liverwurst is good for you. So what if the car leaks more oil than it did when you first took it in. Luigi's got a cold and the car needs an oil change anyway. It doesn't matter if the plumber's bill is $107.89 for three minutes of work. Now that the leak is fixed, just how much is your peace of mind worth anyway?

And they always say yes. They always say no. Actually, they say anything you like if it makes you feel better.

These people can only be properly understood by asking them, Why the aversion to the unpleasant realities that are an integral part of life? It isn't that these people do not find conflict or unpleasantness distressing, as most of us do. It is just that they cannot acknowledge conflict or unpleasantness at all. Why? Usually, because they doubt themselves, but not in the way most people doubt themselves at one time or another. It is much more fundamental than that. It's a complete lack of experience or ability in responding to conflict realistically. Because of that lack of experience or ability, they really have no idea what to do to respond to conflict. Asking them to respond to conflict or unpleasantness openly and constructively is like asking most of us to jump off a ten-story building and then fly down to the ground. We just don't know how to do that. And because we don't, most of us just won't jump off a ten-story building — it is simply too dangerous.

For these people, the primary dangers in responding to conflict probably include being completely overwhelmed by the conflict and making an utter fool of themselves, allowing their own feelings of conflict and anger to show and maybe get out of control, running the risk of looking off balance and out of control to those around them, and allowing others to see parts of their personalities that they are ashamed of or fear. The result of any of these fears, quite naturally, is simply to deny the existence of conflict and unpleasantness. Like most forms of avoidance, such a solution provides immediate relief from the stress of the moment but precludes long-term growth in the areas that are chronically avoided.

A Coping Alternative

The Walt Disney Productions style of avoidance presents an interesting paradox. By denying the problems that you fear, you support their very existence! As long as problems — personal or interpersonal — are avoided, they can never be resolved. Coping requires the understanding that acknowledging problems is the first step to overcoming them.

Facing your fears is the very purpose for which you were

placed on earth. Therein lies growth. Your success in this life will be measured by the degree to which you can face your fears and individual problems, not by your ability to act as if they didn't exist. As therapists and ecclesiastical leaders, we have seen people grow immeasurably by confronting their most difficult problems. Remarkably enough, people are usually grateful to have such problems finally brought out in the open. Furthermore, most people are grateful when we are willing to talk about a problem that might exist between us and them. Precious energy can now be spent in resolving uncomfortable differences rather than in avoiding them. By facing difficult issues you demonstrate strength and courage, both of which are self-approving, both of which increase self-esteem.

It's Written in the Rule Book

Users of the style of avoidance called It's Written in the Rule Book have an overwhelming need to be in charge and have everything done by the book. In their minds, there is a rule for everything. All they have to do is look it up. This attitude is very convenient. If you ever disagree with them, they can look it up and quote you section and paragraph. That procedure makes it evident that you are wrong because the rule is written somewhere. Furthermore, they are right, not because they said so, but because the book said so. This vicarious style of rightness precludes such people from having to take responsibility for their decisions or behavior. As long as it's a rule, there's nothing they can do about it. And if it's not written somewhere, they know they've heard it somewhere before. The point is, there's a rule out there for everything, and they are only playing by the rules.

As long as there are rules, rulers can assure themselves of never losing control. And that's what it's all about: control over self, control over others. Rules provide convenient guidelines in a nasty world that is unruly and disorderly. People can be that way, too: spontaneous, unique, and totally out of order. Rules keep everything in place. Rulers live to maintain order lest by losing control they wind up having to face the things they try so hard to control: themselves and their own fears and sense of inadequacy. People and events must remain predictable and therefore controllable. Deep down inside rulers feel that if things do get out of control, their inadequacies will overpower them and the universe will fall apart. Thus they avoid facing their fears by controlling their environment as much as possible. They also avoid taking responsibility for their overbearing need for control by placing the responsibility on rules that may or may not exist.

A Coping Alternative

Like Walt Disney Productions, there is a fascinating paradox imbedded in this style. To have true control over your life, you must be willing to give up the control you perceive you require. Controlling others to feel good about yourself betrays your own lack of internal control and approval. By remaining rule-bound at the expense of allowing your unique self to contribute to your environment and to those around you, you never afford yourself the opportunity to test the mettle you are truly made of. Failing to know how strong, self-disciplined, or capable you really are forces you to maintain the false boundaries that rules made by others provide. Coping requires that you create your own motives for obeying rules and, where necessary, create your own rules and take ownership of them. Only then can you acknowledge where you are weak and can improve yourself and where you are strong and can help others.

More Avoidance Techniques

Avoidance routines are by no means limited to the five you have read about. A complete list of them is not possible here, but a sample of some of the more impressive routines is listed below. Two things about this list should be noted. First, each of the interpersonal games or strategies helps people avoid conflict and anxiety. Second, when the games are executed with skill and daring, their success is remarkable. Almost all of the following styles of conflict avoidance are discussed more fully by Eric Berne in his book entitled *Games People Play* (New York: Ballantyne Books, 1976) and in Virginia Satir's book on marital relations, *Peoplemaking* (Palo Alto, Calif.: Science and Behavior Books, 1976).

If It Weren't for You

If It Weren't for You (IWFU) is probably the game most commonly played between spouses. Variations of IWFU are played by students who don't apply themselves to their studies and then blame poor grades on their church callings or on roommates whom they've helped through a personal struggle. Children also play IWFU by blaming their failures on parents. IWFU takes on many variations of the scenario played out in the following example:

Mrs. White often complains that her husband restricts her social activities. She tells him, for example, "If it weren't for you, I would have learned to dance." Eventually, Mr. White allows his wife to sign up for dance lessons. At her first dance lesson, Mrs. White finds that she has a terrible fear of dancing in front of others and leaves the room before the first waltz is over.

Mrs. White, the player who is "it" in this game, uses IWFU to avoid facing her own fears. She blames her failure to participate in feared activities on her domineering husband. She even makes him feel guilty about his role in the game so that she not only avoids feared activities but receives gifts and favors from her husband, who tries to make up for his dominance. With her friends, Mrs. White plays a variation of IWFU called

If It Weren't for Him, in which she and her friends blame their lack of accomplishments on their husbands.

Mr. White's participation in the game is also avoidance. He may fear abandonment by his wife. Rather than come to terms with his fear, he demands that his wife rarely leave home, so that he can be sure she cannot abandon him.

Schlemiel and Schmaltz

Schlemiel and Schmaltz is a game often played between two people who could easily be friends, who may even feel they should be friends, but who are afraid of taking the psychological risk of initiating meaningful interchange. The term *schlemiel* comes from a Yiddish word for cunning and refers to people who manage to get their way with other people without conflict. The role of schlemiel is often played by people who need reassurance. They feel irresponsible, so they act irresponsible where they are sure of being told, "That's fine." *Schmaltz* comes from a Yiddish word meaning, literally, "rendered fat." This term refers to the other people in this scenario, who feel put upon but who also feel they must rise above a confrontation in order to win, as in the following example:

Mark and John go to a party. During the course of the evening, they join with some others in a trivia game. At one point, John is about to correctly answer a question and win the game for his team. Mark shouts out the answer from the sidelines, making the question void. John's initial reaction is anger, but he vaguely realizes that if he expresses his anger, he will come off as a sore loser and Mark will win.

Mark says, "I'm sorry. I got carried away."

John mutters, "Oh, that's fine."

Later, John and Mark are conversing with a few others. Mark makes a cutting remark, hitting a sensitive nerve in John. John is offended and wants either to defend himself or to attack Mark.

Mark says, "I'm sorry. I was just joking."

John musters up his good manners and self-control and says, "That's fine."

This behavior continues for the rest of the night.

Mark spills punch on John and says, "I'm sorry. It was an accident."

"That's fine," says John.

Mark makes advances to John's date. "I'm sorry. I was just being sociable."

"That's fine."

Both players, Mark the Schlemiel and John the Schmaltz, completely avoid facing a conflict. Mark is childishly destructive but avoids being forced to truly justify his conduct to others or himself. John avoids the potential embarrassment of a confrontation or of losing his temper but resents Mark and feels cowardly.

See What You Made Me Do

See What You Made Me Do (SWYMMD) is a game people play to avoid other people and also to avoid directly addressing why they want to avoid them. Feeling unsociable or just needing some personal space, they engross themselves in a solitary activity. An intruder, perhaps a child, spouse, or friend comes seeking attention or just to ask a question like "Have you seen the rubber cement?" This interruption "causes" them to forget a line they were writing, or drop the screwdriver, or make an error in calculating, and they yell in anger, "See what you made me do!"

If this game is played often enough, the intruders soon learn to keep their distance. Of course, the people who play SWYMMD are upset by the intruder, not by the "mistake" caused by the interruption, but they are only too happy to use the "mistake" as an excuse to eject the intruder. They play SWYMMD to avoid the difficulty of telling friends or family that they would rather not see them for a while. They may even avoid admitting to themselves that at times they would rather be alone than help others.

Another form of SWYMMD is used to avoid personal responsibility, as in the following example:

Will has difficulty making decisions, so he defers many decisions to his wife, often under the guise of gallantry or democracy. He courteously lets her decide where they will go for dinner or what movie they will see. He finds safety in his decision not to decide. If his wife's choice turns out to be a good one, all is well. If not, he can say, "See what you made us do." Either way he is safe.

The game becomes more serious when played with serious subjects like finances and child-raising. Will lets his wife decide how their accounts will be managed and their children disciplined. Then, if he bounces a check or a child becomes unruly, he can say, "See what you made me do."

At the office, Will asks his subordinates for advice on a project. When the project fails, he blames their input. He asks for their input on his next project, but they wisely say they have no ideas for him. He then asks his superiors for advice. They make several suggestions, which he uses. When this project fails, he says, "See what you made me do." They dismiss him from the company.

People play this form of SWYMMD to avoid facing their inability to make decisions. They avoid risking responsibility for their own actions. They also avoid the intimacy and cooperation necessary to make joint decisions or reach consensus.

Chances are very good that you've seen people use these styles or play these games many times before. Although our descriptions of avoidance may seem humorous, these techniques can be deadly, choking off positive self-evaluative thoughts, which are essential to self-esteem. When avoidance is used to win, look good, or protect our false sense of self, negative self-evaluations and low self-esteem are the inevitable results. Paradoxically, negative self-evaluations and low self-esteem are the very things that avoidance was used to guard against—and ended up fostering instead.

Finding Your Own Coping Responses

Regardless of the avoidance myth you believe in or the avoidance style you adopt or the avoidance game you play, they are all consistently associated with weakness and inadequacy. Coping, on the other hand, is associated with courage and adequacy. The following exercise may be useful in helping you adopt a coping response, no matter what means of avoidance you have employed in the past:

1. Find a quiet, comfortable place where you can be alone and either lie down or sit comfortably. Close your eyes and re-create in your mind a specific and chronic problem that you have avoided facing. Be sure to pick a problem that is of some importance to you.

2. With that specific problem in mind, relive as clearly and as vividly as you can the things you did to avoid dealing with it. Picture all the people involved, the words they spoke, the feelings you had, and, most important, what you did to avoid facing the situation. Think of all the unexpressed feelings or thoughts you had while you were avoiding the situation. Replay the entire experience as if you were watching a video, rewinding it, and watching it all again. Do that three times.

3. When you have finished, think of three adjectives that most accurately describe how you feel about yourself for the way you saw yourself in this scene. Make sure you find words that describe *you*, not how you felt about the event, what happened, or how things turned out because of it. Start with "I saw myself as _____" and then complete the sentence. Write down the three adjectives.

4. With your eyes closed, relive the avoiding scene, but this time, picture yourself acting as if you were the type of person you want to be. Rather than avoid the problem, you are now facing it. Play this coping scenario three times over in your mind, again observing your own behavior and the behavior of others while acknowledging any feelings, thoughts, or impressions you may have.

5. Now think of three adjectives that most accurately describe how you feel about yourself for the way you acted in this coping scene. Write those three words next to the avoidance words.

6. Read your avoidant list out loud. Begin by saying, "When I avoid, I am _____," and then read the three avoidant adjectives. Ask yourself how you feel about yourself when you act that way.

7. Read your coping list out loud. Begin by saying, "When I cope, I am _____," and then read the three coping adjectives. Ask yourself how you feel about yourself when you act that way.

Chances are that you'd much rather have the feelings about yourself that coping brings. Yet in order to cope, you must have a strong understanding of how you avoid. You must be able to recognize it each time you choose to avoid and then acknowledge that avoiding is what you are doing. Find the words that describe you in the process of avoiding and ask yourself how you feel about yourself for being that way. When the discomfort of feeling negatively about yourself for avoiding outweighs the initial fear of trying to cope, your desire to cope will increase. And with each coping response you make, you will find that your self-esteem is growing.

Case Study: Jim

The following example of fear-motivated avoidance and then of coping responses is a good illustration of all the general principles we have been discussing:

It was a golden opportunity. A major studio had liked his proposal for a documentary screenplay and was now requesting the first draft. At age thirty-four, Jim had a chance to expand his career beyond his job as an in-house writer for a large corporation. This chance was something he'd been waiting for. It was the first occasion where his abilities would be pushed to the limit. In spite of his excitement in the face of such good fortune, only one thought came to mind. He would have to produce materials that would be reviewed by experts who would know what he was capable, or incapable, of doing. The thought proved incapacitating.

Jim really wasn't surprised. In fact, this reaction was old hat. Every time he had a chance to do something professionally rewarding, he reacted the same way—he froze. He was well aware that his fear of "going for it" was tied to his fear of failure, in this case, the fear that his best efforts would be found lacking. In spite of his ambition and hunger for success, his attempts at productive work were continually interrupted by television, menial tasks around the house, and other inconsequential activities. Ignoring the critical, he would deal with the mundane, talking himself into believing each silly chore was paramount. Though he had considerable creative and intellectual talents, they remained essentially unused. Better never to try than to be found inadequate in an authentic test. To this day, Jim's manuscript remains only partially completed. What is finished is excellent, and the studio remains eager for him to complete his assigned task, one that will probably never be completed.

By getting the studio interested but then only partially completing the screenplay, Jim again demonstrated to himself the inadequacy of his talents in such a way that his own estimation cannot be refuted by others.

As you might suspect, a life of mediocre accomplishments and personal dissatisfaction is the only realistic outcome for such people, as long as they continue to avoid facing their irrational and unresolved fear of failure. Again, the paradox is evident: avoiding fears in hopes of warding off discomfort, only to endure even more discomfort instead.

About ten months later, Jim had come to a virtual standstill. The screenplay remained on his shelf, and work on it became more and more dissatisfying. An older associate recognized Jim's talent as well as his tendency to underuse it. During lunch and on breaks they spent many hours talking about Jim's fear of failure and how he avoided situations where his fear could be potentially realized. That was the first time anyone had ever explicitly described to him what he really already knew but was never willing to face. Hearing it and understanding it made it more difficult not to do something about it.

In a bid to alter his avoidant style, Jim re-enrolled in a graduate program he had started and — as with other important things — had never finished. He completed his course work and had only one requirement to complete in order to graduate. That one requirement was his master's thesis. Nevertheless, on the eve of imminent success, the fear of failure loomed large once more.

In the face of that specific, crucial task, Jim again started to show the familiar signs of avoidance. He went to his friend, asking what he should do. Somehow he felt that if he could talk some more or in his own words, "get psyched up," he could find the necessary motivation to complete his thesis. His friend listened to his story patiently and attentively, as was his custom. When Jim had finished, the older man sat in silence, pondering the problem. Then, without warning, he confronted Jim with the obvious reality that he didn't seem to really want to complete his thesis, and he was puzzled why he pretended he did. In spite of Jim's protestations to the contrary, the friend shook his head and said he would feel more comfortable with

Jim if he stopped making excuses for what was obvious to them both: he didn't really WANT to finish his thesis, and he was probably afraid to try.

Frustrated and discouraged, Jim stood up to leave, telling his friend that he had been of no help to him and that he felt let down by him. The friend smiled and told Jim to sit back down. He said, "It sounds as though you're your own man with this one. I can't seem to provide you the help you seem to need, though I wish I could. And you don't seem able to get past this barrier on your own. Perhaps it's time to accept the possibility you simply won't be able to finish your thesis."

With that comment, all Jim's rationalizations ceased, as did his attempts to find reassurance from the words of his wiser friend. In the absence of these defenses, his acute personal disapproval of himself for not even trying far exceeded his fear of attempting the task and failing. He had no further recourse but to squarely face that he felt deeply inadequate to the task. He decided that if he could not complete his thesis, he probably couldn't complete anything else of importance either. He now understood and accepted that reality—but more important, he took responsibility for his own failures. His thesis had become the *explicit* test of his adequacy, something that he had always known on an implicit level. What Jim once only acknowledged on the inside, he now recognized on the outside. But with his strength no longer sapped by avoidance and false pretenses and the meaning of the test clear, there was no more denying his fear of failure and avoiding the test of his adequacy. It became much more important to him to see what kind of work he could actually produce.

Jim's friend smiled and nodded his head. He applauded the younger man's honesty and said that if it turned out he couldn't finish his thesis, at least he should "go down fighting the whole way." If he didn't, he would be disappointed in him. He would rather see him give his maximum effort and fail than see him get by with another partial effort. Not once did he reassure Jim that merely by trying he would succeed.

Jim's efforts were well rewarded. He completed his thesis and received an unusual number of compliments from the faculty. Far more important, he had taken the first major step in removing his incapacitating fear of failure. The small confidence in himself he had acquired was well earned. He is now a much closer approximation of the free-lance writer he always wanted to be. Though his accomplishments are still few, his sense of personal well-being has increased measurably and is fairly obvious to those who know him.

We suspect that Jim's improved well-being is not a result of his modest success, though it undoubtedly helped. Rather, it is a result of the self-respect he feels for coping with a major personal conflict instead of avoiding it. As a result of that coping, he has acquired some realistic reasons to believe that he can trust his talents and abilities when he needs them. He has also come to understand the personal cost of avoiding rather than facing conflict. These two elements are major ingredients in his new definition of himself—the influence of which will probably be undeniable in many future events.

In effect, Jim now has a new measuring stick by which to judge his behavior. Knowing and demonstrating that he can face his fears will in the future make it more explicit and undeniable if he fails to do so. He will not be able to rationalize or justify his avoidant behavior with the same ease as he once did. He will have to acknowledge his avoidant behavior for what it is and experience the negative self-evaluations that accompany such avoidance. On the other hand, with each coping response, accompanied by self-approval and positive self-evaluations, Jim's coping behavior will progressively increase.

Coping with threatening situations rather than avoiding them is the means by which individuals can create personal learning experiences that teach about the self and its diverse abilities, liabilities, and needs. Knowledge about the self, when properly acquired, becomes the basis for us to orchestrate our lives into a meaningful, satisfying, and self-directed experience for which we readily accept personal responsibility. In fact, *coping* refers more to a process that regulates realistic learning about the self than it does to any specific psychological quality, attribute, or achievement.

Coping is a growth process in which personal development is the inevitable result of facing, understanding, and resolving conflicts. As a result of accepting higher than usual levels of psychological risk and personal responsibility inherent in the process of psychological coping, we can reasonably expect to experience the following four conditions:

1. The immediate relief of tension and the temporary absence of stress associated with fleeing from conflict will frequently be replaced by uncomfortable feelings of fear or anxiety as we attempt to expose ourselves to problems that we typically avoid. That discomfort should be expected, planned for, and considered perfectly normal in the process of personal growth and development.

2. As we make a strategic shift from avoiding to coping, there will be a corresponding shift in the timing and levels of personal distress in our lives. The long-term debilitating effects of avoidance and low self-esteem will gradually dissipate as we start coping with problems that we typically avoid. Paradoxically, however, coping initially produces rather high levels of immediate and short-term distress. Avoidance tends to produce immediate and short-term relief from distress but guarantees long-term distress and, therefore, low self-esteem. In brief, coping replaces short-term relief and long-term debilitation with short-term distress and long-term growth. Avoidance is fly now and pay later, whereas coping is pay now and fly later.

3. Learning how to face and resolve internal personal prob-

lems and conflicts is a primary way of developing and strengthening the personal traits and emotional strength necessary to cope successfully with our complex social environment with skill, integrity, and candor.

4. When our self-image is a result of personal experience in forthrightly facing and coping with what we fear, we will find our self-image to be both realistic and well-founded. This internal strength will usually manifest itself in the form of self-confidence and self-reliance that is neither arrogant nor superficial. It is the simple result and expression of a carefully nurtured internal sense of personal well-being.

Chapter Seven

Cultivating Spirituality

Cultivating spirituality is usually not something automatic or easy for most people. The path of spiritual development is usually uneven and difficult—a burst of knowledge here, a personal setback there, a recommitment to do better—with our efforts being periodically blessed and sustained by the Lord. It is a continuous struggle to grasp and understand what we can glimpse but seldom hold in clear and constant focus. For many, there are greater problems along the way. Doubts creep in that, if not properly resolved, can leave us spiritually debilitated. The demands and responsibilities of the secular world distract us and consume our time. We become alienated from the saving doctrines of the gospel because we misunderstand them or we don't fully recognize the retarding effects our "minor" sins may have on our spiritual development. And even when we master those problems, there are still others to be considered. A healthy and serious attempt at cultivating enduring, authentic spirituality must frankly acknowledge and then overcome two obstacles.

The first obstacle to spirituality is the natural man, who is instinctively inclined to resist or be unresponsive to the mellow enticings of the Spirit. Pride, self-sufficiency, and striving for invulnerability seem to reside naturally where humility and contrition are required. Although we may regret that state of affairs, it is hardly controversial. More than seventy-five scriptures speak to this point either directly or indirectly. Two of the better known passages are the following: "For the natural man is an enemy to God, and has been from the fall of Adam, and will be, forever and ever, unless he yields to the enticings of the Holy Spirit, and putteth off the natural man and becometh a saint through the atonement of Christ the Lord, and becometh as a child, submissive, meek, humble, patient, full of love, willing to submit to all things which the Lord seeth fit to inflict upon him, even as a child doth submit to his father" (Mosiah 3:19). "We have learned by sad experience that it is the nature and disposition of almost all men, as soon as they get a little authority, as they suppose, they will immediately begin to exercise unrighteous dominion" (D&C 121:39).

Spirituality won't just happen for many people. The passage of time won't create it, neither will maturity, the good wishes of our leaders, nor regular attendance at our meetings. Much more is required. The development of spirituality means the pursuit of eternal truth and knowledge. It is a personal and volitional struggle to learn and implement the will of God in our lives. Our willingness to engage in that struggle is as essential to spiritual development as learning how to recognize and choose good over evil. It is a proactive process of wanting and reaching with consistency and integrity. It is a formidable undertaking and should be accepted as nothing less.

The second obstacle to developing spirituality that we must acknowledge and overcome is more subtle but equally important. That problem is our culturally acquired habit of investing our time and energies in activities whose rewards are the most obvious, immediate, and appealing. The driving force behind our materialism is a "fly now and pay later" mentality.

Principles are secondary to profits and expediency, and immediate gratification is the most important consideration.

Both of these culturally acquired habits are dangerous enemies to us in the pursuit of spiritual truth and knowledge. The more fundamental a gospel teaching, the more likely its enduring, eternal nature will run contrary to the immediacy and practicality that are staple values in our worldly existence. In our search for spiritual truth, sacrifice and study will almost always precede understanding; and enduring principles will hardly ever be affected by short-term expediency. Meaningful truth, whether spiritual or scientific, hardly ever reveals its intimate and powerful secrets to the impatient and impulsive.

So we must wonder how we are to cultivate an abiding spirituality when so many of the forces in the world we live in conspire to confuse and distract us. Our answer can only come from the scriptures. It is illustrated in its alarming simplicity at the conclusion of one of the most eloquent and faith-promoting discourses given to man by a prophet. In this story of conversion, belief, and subsequent spiritual growth, King Benjamin's people "all cried with one voice, saying: Yea, we believe all the words which thou hast spoken unto us; and also, we know of their *surety and truth,* because of the *Spirit of the Lord Omnipotent, which has wrought a mighty change in us, or in our hearts,* that we have no more disposition to do evil, but to do good continually. And we, ourselves, also through the infinite goodness of God, and the manifestations of his Spirit, . . . are willing to enter into a covenant with our God to do his will, and to be obedient to his commandments in all things that he shall command us, all the remainder of our days" (Mosiah 5:2–3, 5; emphasis added). On that day when the Spirit of the Lord encompassed King Benjamin's people, they received an exquisitely clear understanding of the truth. Then, because of the Spirit's revealing the truth, a mighty change was wrought in their hearts. That change of heart coincides with the metaphors pointed out in Chapter 3 of this book, which we described as being synonymous with spirituality. As a result of their change of heart, the people of King Benjamin chose to enter into a covenant to obey God for the remainder of their days, a thing which they would not have done without knowing the truth and their hearts being changed.

There we have the scriptural blueprint for cultivating spirituality. We suggest that cultivating spirituality in today's world involves the same considerations as it did in the days of King Benjamin: seeking and receiving an understanding of the truth, undergoing a mighty change of heart, and then acting upon that truth which we have received.

Seeking and Receiving an Understanding of Truth

Things as They Really Are

There are numerous ways of defining what the truth is. We have found Elder Neal A. Maxwell's definition to be most elegant, direct, and enduring. He begins by quoting from Jacob 4:13:

" 'Behold, my brethren, he that prophesieth, let him prophesy to the understanding of men; for the Spirit speaketh the truth and lieth not. Wherefore, it speaketh of things as they really are, and of things as they really will be.' . . .

"Jacob's declaration about truth is, of course, consistent with the definition of truth given by the Lord to a later prophet, Joseph Smith: 'And truth is knowledge of things as they are, and as they were, and as they are to come.' (D&C 93:24.) . . .

"The true religionist is actually the ultimate realist, for he has a fully realistic view of man and the universe; he traffics in truths that are culminating and everlasting; he does not focus on facts that fade with changing circumstance or data that dissolve under pressures of time and circumstance. The Lord said, ' . . . truth abideth and hath no end.' (D&C 88:66.)" (*Things As They Really Are* [Salt Lake City: Deseret Book Co., 1978], p. 1).

Truth, then, is things as they really are. If truth prevailed in its purest sense in this impure world, the true nature of all things would be known. There would be no pretense, pretext, or prevarication. There would be no need for argument, because opinion would be based on the truth—a truth that all could see. Subjectivity and objectivity would be one and the same. We would see all things as they really are, and we would know each other as we really are.

The truth simply is. It can neither be created nor destroyed. In the Doctrine and Covenants we read that, "All truth is independent in that sphere in which God has placed it" (D&C 93:30). This passage implies that the nature of truth remains constant regardless of time, circumstance, or perception. The scriptures, for instance, are truth. Although people attempt to destroy, dishonor, or discredit them, the scriptures in their independent sphere will remain what they are: the word of the Lord, forever.

Things as They Seem to Be

It must be admitted that human understanding of "true things" will always be limited and slightly distorted. That is as true of scientific propositions and facts as it is of religious concepts and practices. Truth is revealed by knowledge, and we gain knowledge through our various senses. Those senses are seldom the perfect receivers we would like them to be. So, as noble as mankind's pursuit of truth is, whether it be scientific or spiritual, we must understand that our comprehension of truth, our ability to accurately perceive the uncontaminated truth, is limited and partially impaired. Until we are in a more perfect state, much of what we now understand can only be considered approximations to the ultimate truths that can be known after the resurrection. With that in mind, several precautions prove useful in our individual search for spiritual truth during our mortal existence:

1. Personal wants and wishes regularly influence (distort) how we perceive things. The fact that our personal wants and wishes are real (true), does not alter the fact that they can distort how we perceive other, more fundamental, truths.

2. Social and cultural demands and rewards regularly influence (distort) how we perceive things. Even though the cultural influences may or may not be of our choosing, that does not alter the fact that they regularly determine what we consider to be true as well as how we respond to it.

3. Situational stress and the demands of the moment can exert powerful influences on what we are willing to accept as the truth. Regrettably, these are the conditions under which people's self-serving motives (distortions) are least likely to be recognized for what they are.

In brief, the process of human perception is an active one. The values, preferences, and needs of perceivers often become part of the very event they are trying to perceive with clarity and precision. The implications of this statement are far-reaching. A seeker of truth must understand that whereas the truth is constant, our perceptions of it probably are not. Furthermore, many distortions of truth are self-made and self-serving, and obstacles to seeing things as they really are can only be properly compensated for by acknowledging the fallibility of our own perceptions. Acknowledging and accepting our own fallibility is essential to our moving closer to truth's infallibility. Humility and faith must flourish where certainty is generally preferred.

The following story illustrates how personal wants and needs seductively distort our perceptions of truth without our even knowing it:

A young man went to his bishop about a persistent and long-standing sexual sin. He requested a blessing immediately

117

upon entering the bishop's office, asserting that that was the only way he could be helped. The bishop listened for a moment and concluded privately that a blessing would not be appropriate. Instead, he chose to listen to the young man in order to gain further insight into the problem.

As the young man disclosed the details of his nearly debilitating problem, a recurring theme was evident: the young man had abandoned all hope and no longer believed it was in his power or ability to deal with the problem on his own. The bishop was confused about his initial impression and wondered if this was a problem over which the young man could still exercise volitional control. The compelling and persuasive details of the young man's story required the bishop to re-evaluate his earlier impression to not give a blessing. Eventually, he decided to give a blessing after all.

The blessing was short, succinct, and undeniable. Much to the surprise of both the bishop and the young man, without the slightest pause the bishop pronounced that the young man was an agent unto himself. It was already within his power to abstain from his indiscretions, if he would choose to do so. In the eyes of the Lord he was accountable for all of his past indiscretions and those he might yet commit.

Things as they really are became exquisitely clear both to the bishop and to the young man. In this situation, this young man was free to exercise his will in spite of his protestations to the contrary. Now the young man understood that he had a much more serious problem than he had originally supposed. He left the bishop's office understanding that he now had to face and resolve some unpleasant realities about his "willful" nature that he had previously avoided by claiming helplessness.

Seeing Things as They Really Are

The difficulty we face is learning how to see things as they really are despite our own tendency to distort the truth as well

as our willingness to be satisfied with less than the truth.
Because of that simple reality, the first step in cultivating spirituality—searching for things as they really are—must necessarily
be a process of looking beyond appearances. That can be
difficult. It is certainly tempting to accept the false fronts and
superficial standards of counterfeit truth. Because they are so
abundant and bear a strong surface resemblance to their authentic counterparts, they are often easily mistaken for the real
things. Furthermore, embracing the obvious and ordinary is
infinitely easier than struggling to reach beyond what is so
readily within our reach. We must, therefore, resist being satisfied with half-hearted attempts or first-try results. To know
the truth, to know things as they really are, requires a greater
diligence and stretching that may trouble and try us. In the
words of Elder John A. Widtsoe, "A conviction of the truth of
the gospel, a testimony, must be sought if it is to be found. It
does not come as the dew from heaven. It is the result of man's
eagerness to know truth. Often it requires battle with traditions,
former opinions and appetites, and a long testing of the gospel
by every available fact and standard. . . .

"All should test their religious beliefs. But all such testing
must be done in the right spirit and by the right method. Every
testing must be a sincere and honest search for truth" (*Evi-
dences and Reconciliations*, 2d ed. [Salt Lake City: Bookcraft,
1943], pp. 6, 23).

How, then, do we overcome the human problems of distorting truth and failing to recognize it when we see it?

The resolution may appear difficult, but it is not complex.
Within each one of us exists the ability to discern truth. That
ability comes from our own innate, eternal nature. That nature
is part intelligence, which is the "light and truth" that was with
God in the beginning (D&C 93:29). Because of its penetrating
and transcendant character, our eternal nature is the only
means whereby we can differentiate between what may appear

to be spiritual and what really is spiritual. The capacity to discern light and truth is the essence of our eternal identity.

Our own eternal nature, then, is both a detector and a receptor of truth. It is partially the result of being begotten by the Father and partially the result of being with the Father in the beginning, before the Creation. It is the essence of what we are. And that part of us is not passive. It resonates with truth, it seeks truth, it rejoices in the presence of truth, and it is most fully activated by the light and truth that emanates from Christ, who personifies truth. The light within us, when activated by the light of Christ, has its own unique radiance. Learning to feel and respond to spiritual radiance is the key to spiritual development.

So, how do we learn to feel the light of Christ radiating to our eternal self and from our eternal self to our mortal self, particularly when the glow is subtle? We can learn through many different things—prayer, fasting, scripture study, blessings, and seeking righteousness. But in another sense, we always learn through the same thing: attending to, cultivating, differentiating, and then trusting our spiritual identity that receives the light and truth that emanate from Christ. The spiritual person must be shaped and influenced by spiritual forces from within.

So far, we have described a process of spiritual development that focuses on the internal/eternal identity. We have repeatedly pointed out that the very essence of that identity is spiritual and naturally resonates with the light and truth that emanates from Christ. But we have said virtually nothing about the processes that activate the receptor of truth. That is an important consideration, particularly in light of the morally bankrupt world that surrounds us and influences us. We must consider how and why spiritual influences can affect our lives in an environment that can be so alien to them. Following are several possibilities:

1. There are times that the Lord simply overpowers us, and we are initially brought to an awareness of his spiritual presence in spite of ourselves or our worthiness.

2. The Church has never been ambiguous about the importance of studying the scriptures and praying as a way of developing spirituality in our lives.

3. Missionaries, teachers, parents, leaders, and others who are authentically moved by the Spirit can introduce to others the feelings that accompany the presence of the Spirit simply because others can feel its presence through them.

4. We have all been blessed with the light of Christ, which allows us to discern good and evil if we are truly interested in doing so.

5. Priesthood ordinances such as baptism, the gift of the Holy Ghost, and blessings are frequently the means by which individuals come to a fuller awakening of their spiritual capacities.

6. And, finally, an abiding sense of spirituality is probably a natural consequence of humbling ourselves because we love the Lord and understand the scriptures. This point is made clear in Alma 32:14: "And now, as I said unto you, that because ye were compelled to be humble ye were blessed, do ye not suppose that they are more blessed who truly humble themselves because of the word?"

The paramount importance of a deep sense of personal humility in developing spirituality is further indicated by Christ's declaring that his life and atonement fulfilled the law of Moses (3 Nephi 9:17). Then the Savior said: "And ye shall offer up unto me no more the shedding of blood; yea, your sacrifices and your burnt offerings shall be done away, for I will accept none of your sacrifices and your burnt offerings. And ye shall offer for a sacrifice unto me a broken heart and a contrite spirit. And whoso cometh unto me with a broken heart and a contrite spirit, him will I baptize with fire and with the Holy Ghost" (3 Nephi 9:19–20).

It is apparent that humility, a broken heart, and a contrite spirit are the precise conditions under which we are the most receptive to the truth about our own sinful nature and the most aware of our absolute reliance on repentance and the Atonement for our salvation. The significance of humility in our spiritual development is made clear in Ether 12:27: "And if men come unto me I will show unto them their weakness. I give unto men weakness that they may be humble; and my grace is sufficient for all men that humble themselves before me; for if they humble themselves before me, and have faith in me, then will I make weak things become strong unto them."

So you see, heightened spirituality is not the result of willpower and discipline (forms of self-reliance), though will-power and discipline play a prominent role in cultivating humility through study of the scriptures, prayer, and so forth. Humility is more the result of seeing ourselves as we really are, with all of our mortal foibles, and clearly seeing God's love for us as it really is. Perceiving these fundamental truths in their simplicity is the beginning of appreciation and humility. Paradoxically, it is that humility within us that plays such an important role in arousing the spiritual capacities that also reside within us.

Undergoing a Mighty Change of Heart

The people of King Benjamin came to understand two fundamental truths on the day of their conversion; they under-stood the truth about their own sinful nature and the truth about the divine nature of Christ. These two truths, juxtaposed, created a comparison far too compelling to ignore. The alter-natives were simple and clear: openly embrace their sinful nature and, in the face of complete understanding, reject Christ; or acknowledge their sinful nature, forsake it, and embrace

Christ. Seeing things as they really are forced the issue, requiring them to decide. When they made that decision, their hearts were changed. Their newborn spiritual state allowed them to see the present and future glory of the Lord.

The change of heart we too must experience for ourselves is similar. Spirituality can be achieved only to the degree that we acknowledge who and what we are. Unless we make such an acknowledgment, the incongruity of who we portray ourselves to be and who we really are will stand in the way of our totally accepting Christ. Maintaining facades, covering up fears, and hiding from weaknesses is denying the truth, a truth we must face in order to face Christ. Facing that truth requires a broken heart and a contrite spirit. They, in turn, replace fear with courage, weakness with strength, incongruity with congruity, and fear with hope.

Acting on That Truth We Have Received: "Give Me All"

The covenant the people of King Benjamin made was not only a consequence of their changed hearts and newfound spirituality but also a reinforcement of their spirituality. Spirituality is not a passive thing. It requires commitment to remain active and alive. Commitment that comes from true spirituality, born of substance and congruence, is synonymous with submitting our individual will to that of the Lord. In so doing, our will and his become one, where at least for one perfect moment, his infinite mind and our finite minds are at once harmonious, consonant, and unified. When that unity happens, our motives for seeking spirituality are not, cannot, be tainted by what is not true. It is impossible to be in harmony with the Lord while in disharmony with ourselves or others. We are able to arrive on that plane of which the Savior spoke when he importuned his Father to make his disciples one "as thou,

Father, art in me, and I in thee, that they also may be one in us" (John 17:21).

Through a broken heart, contrite spirit, and a recognition of truth, we can commit ourselves, out of love, to please the Savior and to serve him by serving others. There are no other reasons for worship; there are no other motives for spirituality. In their absence, self-aggrandizement or self-doubt creep in, and our so-called spiritual exercises serve little more than to spiritually weaken and, ultimately, condemn us.

When we commit to the Savior we must do so fully. In the words of C. S. Lewis, "Christ says, 'Give me All. I don't want so much of your time and so much of your money and so much of your work: I want You. I have not come to torment your natural self, but to kill it. No half-measures are any good. I don't want to cut off a branch here and a branch there, I want to have the whole tree down. I don't want to drill the tooth, or crown it, or stop it, but to have it out. Hand over the whole natural self, all the desires which you think innocent as well as the ones you think wicked—the whole outfit. I will give you a new self instead. In fact, I will give you Myself: my own will shall become yours'" (*Mere Christianity* [London: Collins, 1988], p. 167).

Commitment to the Savior must be both internal and external; otherwise, it is not commitment. Spirituality, too, must be both internal and external, or it is not spirituality. Our level of commitment and spirituality will be manifested by the degree to which we do the right things for the right reasons. No more. No less.

The Greatest Hoax: Incongruity between Appearance and Substance

Much of our discussion has been about truth, about being congruent, about allowing the internal/eternal self to develop and eventually dictate outward behavior so there is little difference between who you really are and who you represent yourself to be. Regrettably, this mortal existence is the perfect breeding ground for the broadest variance between ɪeality and appearance. And, more regrettably, all of us participate in the creation of that hoax and may not even realize it. The human factor can create a deadly form of deception to which we can all fall prey. Let's review how that can happen.

When we are in frequent contact with something, it is difficult to maintain our initial appreciation for it. A good example is the automobile. It is capable of getting us to work in minutes while we sit comfortably and listen to a variety of music or the latest reports on world events, change the temperature to suit our comfort, make phone calls, and carry enough luggage to be gone for a month. Yet the longer we have an automobile, the less we seem to appreciate it. In fact, we seem to appreciate it only when we don't have it.

Taking an automobile for granted may seem unimportant. But when we take for granted the truth of things of the Spirit, we run the risk of a most subtle and serious kind of deception: trivializing what is truly substantial while still acting as if it were important to us. For instance, through repetition and rote we can trivialize prayer, reducing it from a sweet communion to a hollow echo of previous supplications. We can continue acting as if prayer were meaningful by still getting down on our knees at night, blessing the food, or offering invocations in church meetings regardless of an improvised internal spiritual state. Even with the substance gone, we can still continue the semblance. When that happens, we lose the thoughts, the feelings, the resonating with the Spirit that accompany things of the Spirit, yet we continue behaving outwardly as if what we were doing was meaningful, significant, and a reflection of our truest internal self. The deception lies not only in the incongruity between outward appearances and inward substance but also in the willingness to maintain the outward zeal when the inner senses verge on apathy. By refusing to acknowledge the absence of the Spirit, we run the risk of not having the Spirit at all.

How do we remedy that problem of incongruity between outward appearance and inward substance? How do we remove ourselves from the condemning hoax of maintaining the outward zeal when the inner self is apathetic?

Let's go back and take another look at the automobile for a moment. What do we typically do to impress upon our teenage children the grave responsibility they have when they first learn to drive? We raise such issues as how expensive the car is to operate, maintain, and keep insured, how powerful and dangerous two tons of steel can be at sixty-five miles an hour, how they might get a ticket, or have the privilege of driving taken away from them if they abuse it. We teach them specific procedures to follow every time they get behind the wheel: buckle up the seat belt, check the fuel gauge, check the rearview mirror before they pull out—all of which could possibly save their lives some day. We take the concept of the family station wagon sitting in the driveway and broaden its meaning and significance. It is no longer merely a set of wheels that our children have gotten into and out of for half a dozen years. It is now in a context of other people, other cars, and potential hazards as well as potential benefits. It is not just an immediate, ordinary object; it is also a representation of its extraordinary possibilities for both good and bad. In short, a clear, accurate, and continual consciousness of the value, costs, potential dangers, and the inherent responsibilities of those who use the car is all that can prevent the use of the automobile from being trivialized.

If we are going to reduce the risk of making spiritual matters trivial, so too must we keep them in proper perspective. The sacrament provides us an excellent example, especially because the things we have frequent contact with stand a greater chance of being trivialized. If we are to uphold the sacred nature of the sacrament, we must first of all see beyond the ritual we practice each Sunday. The sacrament is not just bread and water. It represents the flesh and blood of Christ. Partaking of the sacramental bread and water represents our renewing the covenants we made at baptism, which is the gateway to salvation. We demonstrate our rebirth in Christ through the waters of baptism. If the meaning of what the sacrament represents is lost, the weekly practice of partaking of it becomes trivial. We no longer view partaking of the sacrament as an ordinance that can spiritually renew or spiritually condemn. It is merely a process that we participate in out of habit, or fear that someone will see us if we don't, or failure to understand how sacred it truly is.

Trivializing spiritual activity is a major stumbling block to cultivating true spirituality. As long as we call activities spiritual when they are not, true spirituality is blocked and frustrated while we remain satisfied with its mere appearance. If we trivialize spiritual activities, we can easily take for granted what could be truly spiritual activities by executing them in a half-hearted way and still calling them spiritual, even though the Spirit is absent. Either way, we have sacrificed spiritual substance for its much more evident, yet empty, form. Elder Neal A. Maxwell describes the trap of superficiality:

"Some give of their time yet withhold themselves, being present without giving of their presence and going through the superficial motions of membership instead of the deep emotions of consecrated discipleship.

"Some try to get by with knowing only the headlines of the gospel, not really talking much of Christ or rejoicing in Christ and esteeming lightly His books of scripture which contain and explain His covenants (see 2 Nephi 25:26)" (*Ensign,* May 1987, p. 70).

The importance of substance in spiritual activities is

evident. Yet, oftentimes, even the substance behind the activity may be motivated out of less than spiritual intent. Here are five common ulterior motives that cannot qualify behavior as spiritual:

1. Striving for spirituality *cannot* be motivated out of a fear of others. If we engage in activities that appear spiritual in order to please and placate others because we fear what they might think or say, fear is the primary motive, not worship or seeking spirituality.

2. Striving for spirituality *cannot* be motivated out of a need to avoid other personal responsibilities. Some individuals increase what appears to be spiritual activity as a means of avoiding legitimate responsibility elsewhere in their lives. The husband who overcommits to quorum duties at the expense of family obligations is a classic example. He is no longer serving the kingdom as much as he is serving himself.

3. Striving for spirituality *cannot* be done at the expense of others. Such is the case of the wife who uses family prayer as a weapon against her husband. He forgets to call the family together so she does it with great impatience, making sure her husband feels guilty or embarrassed in front of the children. Prayer now is the vehicle for a power struggle instead of a means to communicate with the Lord.

4. Striving for spirituality *cannot* be motivated by a need to dominate, control, and subjugate others. The unrighteous father who uses his patriarchal role as an excuse to bully his children or wife is but one example of spiritual trappings disguising other than spiritual motives.

5. Striving for spirituality *cannot* be motivated out of a need for recognition or personal gain. Service cannot be offered as a bid for receiving praise from others. Involvement in meetings through talks and prayers cannot be motivated out of a need to be recognized as someone knowledgeable or pious. In the words of Elder Marlin K. Jensen of the First

Quorum of the Seventy, "Those who seek honor and gain for themselves in doing the Lord's work are guilty of what the scriptures call priestcrafts" (*Ensign,* Nov. 1989, p. 27).

Cultivating spirituality requires carefully assessing our motives for engaging in spiritual activity. Behaviors we once perceived as spiritual may very well be motivated by purposes that hinder the very spirituality being sought. To heighten our awareness of the deception in trivializing spiritual things, the following points may be helpful:

1. When participating in sacred ordinances or other spiritual activities, look beyond the limited behaviors themselves to focus on the limitless meanings and significance the behaviors represent. Keeping the broader perspective, searching for eternal implications in the otherwise mortal motions, is paramount.

2. Consider why we do what we do. Is an action an expression of our internal love of the Lord and charity for others, or are our motives tainted by more self-serving purposes?

3. If outward spiritual activity is accompanied by an inward spiritual emptiness, acknowledging that incongruity to ourselves and then to the Lord alleviates the deception. Acknowledgment can reduce our inclination to increase activity as a way of disavowing that there is a problem; more meeting attendance, more scripture study, more service. While such activity is worthwhile, it cannot replace a broken heart and a contrite spirit. A spiritual problem requires a spiritual remedy. Through fervent prayer we can recognize our weaknesses, which cause spiritual problems. Until that recognition is made, activity void of the Spirit merely covers up such difficulties.

4. Pride precipitated by the fear of *appearing* less than worthy must be done away with in order to become worthy. Abandoning trivial participation in sacred things may be difficult as old habits are replaced with renewed convictions. The

process of cultivating spirituality is one of change: a change of heart, a change of mind, a change of behavior.

The following story illustrates the concepts we have been discussing:

Carl had always done his home teaching as long as he could remember—as a teacher with his dad, as an elder, and now as a high priest. His sense of duty and obligation were strong, and so each month his families could be assured a visit. They weren't remarkable visits. They weren't like the stories you'd hear in church meetings or see on Church videos. They were just visits. He'd wonder every now and then how you could get the Spirit that would make home teaching something more than just friendly chit-chat once a month. He knew he didn't have it. But in its absence, it was enough for him to know that home teaching was something one just did. It gave him some satisfaction to be able to say he'd gotten it done, although sometimes he wondered if it was more a feeling of relief. Either way, his calling was fulfilled, even if it was not magnified.

The habit of home teaching had become a trivial thing to Carl. There was no malicious intent or premeditation involved. It was only a matter of gradually learning over the years to accept home teaching as an activity that could be done without the internal effort of seeking the Spirit. Thus reduced, home teaching was no more than any other passing, friendly gesture. It would never be more until Carl realized that "getting the spirit" of home teaching was not so much something you "got" as it was a process of soul-searching to find out why you *hadn't* got it. As President Spencer W. Kimball taught us a long time ago concerning things of the Spirit, "Learn, then teach." President Ezra Taft Benson made the same point in his book *A Witness and a Warning,* in a chapter entitled "Cleansing the Inner Vessel."

Cultivating spirituality is not easy nor was it meant to be.

Finding the truth, having a change of heart, and then committing ourselves to Christ run contrary to the natural man within us and are, consequently, difficult tasks. Confounded by the tendency to trivialize spiritual things, we may feel that the process of becoming truly spiritual is not merely arduous but impossible.

To get past feeling overwhelmed, we must focus on the word *process*. Much like self-esteem, spirituality cannot be considered an achievement, something we strive for and then receive. It is not something that can be obtained, like a trophy awarded at the finish line and then placed on the mantel for display. Spirituality is the training, the exercise, and the running of the race, regardless of what place we finish in. It is dynamic and fluid. Its nature and strength are contingent upon the process we choose to apply and follow daily.

Rather than adding spirituality to a long list of things to do, make spirituality the template that guides the doing. *What* is done becomes secondary to *how* it is done. Personal accomplishments are much less important than the personal integrity that guides their being done. The character we display, the Christlike qualities we exemplify, become embedded in the choices we make, the relationships we cultivate, and the many small behaviors that make up our larger lives.

Chapter Eight

Spirituality and Self-Esteem:
Putting It All Together

In this concluding chapter we illustrate the process of cultivating spirituality and self-esteem in a practical context. The
case study is one from our own experience. It has been altered
only enough to preserve the individual's privacy and abbreviated enough to be included in this chapter. This case study
provides a real-life context to illustrate the role of self-
evaluative thoughts and feelings and the power of the internal/
eternal identity on the development of self-esteem and spirituality. Note the pervasive influence of impression management,
the style of avoidance James employs, even in childhood, to
keep from having to deal directly with the problem he has
with his height.

Case Study: James

Early Childhood

James was born thirty-seven years ago. His birth was the
fulfillment of his parents' and grandparents' hopes but hardly
a spectacular event for anyone else. The first five years of his
life were typical: breast feeding, potty training, a dozen stitches,

and the birth of a new brother and sister who seemed tolerable to him most of the time. He was loved, played with, spanked occasionally, and generally nurtured in the best traditions of a Latter-day Saint family. He was an "okay" kid whose early development was essentially natural, timely, and orderly.

In the second grade he became aware that he was shorter than the other kids. He first noticed when other kids started calling him Shorty and teased him about his size. Nevertheless, he learned to read, write, count, and ride his bike just like everyone else. He tried to pretend that being small didn't matter very much, but it really did. By the fifth grade there was still no improvement in his comparatively short height. He was growing and maturing, all right, but the other kids were growing faster. He eventually stopped hoping to be as tall as the others and just prayed that he wouldn't stop growing very soon.

He heard all of the reassuring words from sensitive teachers and caring parents, but it didn't help much. It certainly didn't make up for being picked last for most team sports. And that's what clinched it. By the time he was in the fourth grade he had a well-established case of self-consciousness that was primarily an outgrowth of his small stature.

That his younger brother Frankie was twice as big and much more athletic didn't help matters. That was particularly evident when they both wound up on the same peewee league baseball team together. Frankie played a key position on the team, had a great throwing arm, and was a big hitter. He was always noticed and even got his picture in the neighborhood paper once for playing such a good game. James learned to live with it, but it was never easy.

The league rules required that every player have a turn at bat whether he played in the field or not. That alone kept the possibility open that James could one day hit a line drive out of the infield with the winning runs on base. Regrettably, however, James hardly ever hit the ball when it was his turn at bat.

Because of his short stature, few pitchers could throw the ball in the infinitesimally small strike zone he provided, and he almost always drew a walk. Oh well, he at least got to run the bases that way.

One day the team was taking batting practice before a game. James was at bat. The coach was pitching to him. James swung at every pitch and generally made contact with the ball. He was determined to hit that line drive out of the infield even if it was only in batting practice. Right in the middle of his turn, the coach stopped pitching, called the team around him, and asked everyone to take note of how eager James was to hit the ball—how he took a "cut" at every pitch. The coach said he wanted everyone on the team to approach the plate with the same hitting attitude.

Naturally, James was in ecstasy. The coach's comments, though intended for the team, had lifted his self-esteem to the heavens. He felt important. He had been noticed. He was an example of something good. And it felt great. That he walked once and struck out twice in the game was easily overlooked. Praise at last!

Commentary

James, like anyone who is self-conscious and feels inferior, was clearly eager for the approval, recognition, and acceptance of others. That need for acceptance and approval made his teen years particularly difficult. During those years, the stakes of individuality and conformity are much higher. Individuality and self-government run the risk of alienating others—a loss that is seldom affordable by those with low levels of self-esteem. But conformity to the whims and expectations of others is equally risky. Conformity can bring acceptance, but that acceptance depends on allegiance to group values that are seldom congruent with the values or practices of most Latter-day Saint families. And so the battle for self-direction and internal development in this young man's life entered its most crucial stage.

Teens

The teenage years were difficult for James. It was nearly impossible for him to gain peer recognition without compromising the values he'd been raised with. When he could not get the stylish clothes that his peers wore, he was deeply distressed, but his parents simply could not afford them. He worried so much about the bullies at school that he started taking karate lessons. He had only a few very close friends. They were meaningful and satisfying relationships, but they did not include the most popular kids in school. In these close relationships James first discovered that others found his sense of humor very entertaining. His sense of humor started earning him the approval and attention of others he so desperately wanted. It was quite natural, then, that he gradually came to play the role of the clown and joker in most of his relationships.

He graduated from high school with a completely undistinguished academic record, and he stood a full eight inches shorter than he wished to be. He was 5' 4" and he would have given his firstborn child if he could only have been six feet tall. His social circle was restricted to the same friends he had had; he made few if any new friends. His work habits, emotional maturity, and self-esteem were on a par with his physical stature: noticeably below average. His ambitions were limited or absent. But far more disturbing to his parents was his reluctance even to try much of anything other than entertain everybody, which he seemed to do rather well. It didn't look to most observers as if James had much hope for a happy and productive life.

Commentary

The account of James's growing up years is not a hard luck story. He had many advantages that most youth don't. He was loved by his family, cared for and nurtured by his parents, endowed with good health, and had at least an average intelligence. He just happened to be short in a culture that values size and stature, particularly with young males. Consequently, he had to suffer somewhat — not because there was something wrong with him, but because what others thought of him became more important to him than what he thought of himself. The result was low self-esteem, which originates in our cultural conditioning and is common to many youths and adults. In James's case, low self-esteem impaired his ability to recognize and cultivate his own talents and capacities because he was usually investing his time and energy in gaining the approval of others. What was noticeably absent in James's life was self-approval and self-direction, a process that requires higher levels of psychological risk-taking, personal responsibility, and an unfailing sensitivity to the internal self in both psychological and spiritual spheres.

Adulthood

Twenty years after graduating from high school, James is a very successful attorney with a large firm. He graduated second in his law school class and accumulated a number of academic honors and awards along the way. He is an avid sports participant and an accomplished athlete in tennis, golf, basketball, and softball. He has a wide circle of rather intimate friends with whom he shares genuine affection and comfort. He has a wife and four children whom he deeply loves. At work he is competent, respected, and productive. A year ahead of schedule he was made a full partner in the law firm where he works — a clear and unmistakable indication of his professional competence. Almost everyone enjoys his company. He has held positions of responsibility in his church. Accepting those positions is a natural expression of his commitment to Christ, which he acquired on his mission. Even though his level of self-esteem is now unusually high, few would have any way of knowing that without talking with him about personal matters he considers private.

Commentary

Few would have guessed that James had the capacity or disposition necessary for the level of success he enjoys in his life. So now we must ask: "How is it that he changed? And why do some people manage to change successfully while others don't?" And much more specifically, "How did James change, and can anyone change the same way if they really want to?"

Those are important questions! Most people seem to understand intuitively that changing well-established habits is difficult. Some probably consider it impossible. But change does take place regularly. We see it all the time. It comes in different shapes and sizes, but it is still change. We see it during career changes at midlife, in the adjustment process of newlyweds, in the recovering alcoholic, in the recently widowed, in new parents, and in the repentant sinner. In fact, we live in a world of continual change.

So, let's take a careful look at the important principles and critical events that helped James change so much. To do that, we asked James to explain in writing how and in what ways he changed. Before presenting his response, however, we will briefly review the essential principles of perfecting the internal self. They include the self-esteem of the secular person and the spirituality of the eternal person. It is important to remember that even though self-esteem and spirituality represent different domains of mortal experience, their development seems to be regulated by underlying processes that are remarkably similar.

The Development of Self-Esteem

The development of high and low levels of self-esteem is primarily the result of each person's inclination either to cope with or to avoid what they fear. Coping is an inherently self-affirming and self-fulfilling human experience in spite of its difficulty because of the high quality and uniquely human responses it requires. Those responses include the following:

Acknowledging imperfections in the self
Having insight into one's motives
Being honest with self and others
Looking inward to the self and solving problems
Taking psychological risks
Accepting personal responsibility

The very act of psychological avoidance is a self-defeating behavior that precludes high levels of self-esteem because of the inadequacies inherent in avoidance. Those responses include the following:

Denial
Distortion
Rationalization
Fear

The Development of Spirituality

Spirituality, like self-esteem, is an internal quality and tends to develop in those who are humble rather than proud. Spirituality is a powerful self-affirming and self-fulfilling human experience in spite of its difficulty because of the high quality and uniquely spiritual capacities it arouses in us. Humility, and the spirituality humility helps engender, seems to be a product of:

Teachableness
Gratitude
Charity

Personal pride precludes the possibility of a rich and active spiritual life because its underlying components are so alien to things of the Spirit. Those components include the following:

Self-aggrandizement
Self-centeredness
Self-consciousness

In brief, both spirituality and self-esteem are powerful, self-affirming experiences that partially fulfill our unique psychological and spiritual endowments. More importantly, developing spirituality and self-esteem requires us to face and overcome our natural limitations in the respective spheres of influence. In so doing, we engage in the precise process that leads to strengthening and, ultimately, perfecting the internal self. In our view, the internal self, both spiritual and psychological, is where personal government and self-direction must reside during our mortal existence. The internal self is the only part of us that can truly discern truth on a spiritual plane and self-approving behavior patterns on a secular one.

Avoidance and pride simply play no useful role in developing our spiritual or psychological selves. Generally speaking, avoidance and pride represent the lowest levels of human functioning and can properly be considered self-defeating behaviors.

We now invite you to read James's own account of his life experiences. Please notice that the changes were more gradual than sudden and proceeded from internal to external changes that included both spirituality and self-esteem. Remarkably, the internal changes in spirituality and in self-esteem seem to nurture and complement each other. The following is how and why James changed, in virtually his own words.

James Tells His Own Story

Youth: The Power of External Influences

"As I look back on my life, particularly my youth, it is clear that my feelings of self-worth hinged almost entirely on how others treated me. What's more, the feedback I received from others always seemed to affect me far beyond the context in which it was delivered. If a coach complimented me, that didn't just mean I was a good player; it meant that I was 'a heckuva person overall.' The same was true about comments about being small. They always seemed to apply with equal force to areas of my life that were well beyond the scope of their intent. But, most importantly, my feelings about myself were derived almost exclusively from others.

"Not surprisingly, the way others treated me outside my home, no matter how shallow the relationship, was accepted with credibility that was at least equal to the solid reassurance I received from my rather wise and discerning parents. That strikes me as an important point because for most little Latter-day Saint boys, their home may be their castle, but social peers are still likely to be their government. A few examples may illustrate this important point:

"In the fourth grade at recess, my class of twenty or so kids played kickball. The teams were made up by the two best players in the class, Jeff and Tony. They picked one additional person and then took on the rest of the class. Frequently, I was selected to join the dynamic duo and take on the class with them. Notwithstanding my small size, I could kick well and eventually became a regular with Jeff and Tony. To me, that didn't just mean I was a good kickball player. Jeff and Tony were popular because they played kickball well. Now I was popular because they wanted me to play kickball with them. I took that feedback and wore it like a medal of honor all year long. I wore it and thought about it in everything I did —

whether it was following Mom around the grocery store or fishing with Dad. The fact of the matter was that everyone in the class thought that Jeff, Tony, and I were the best kickball players in the class — and that fact was crucial in my own feelings about the kind of person I was.

"In ninth grade I tried out for the basketball team. I was still little, but Dad had put up a basket in our backyard, and I spent a lot of time shooting baskets. Before tryouts, all the guys who wanted to make the team played in the gym after school. If anybody gave me enough room to shoot inside fifteen feet, I was money in the bank. In those little pretryout practice games, guys didn't guard me closely because I was small. I would score five to ten consecutive baskets, and then the other team would assign one of their best players to guard me. He would block the first shot I tried, and within moments my offensive prowess was neutered. But the fact of the matter was, I commanded attention from one of the best players because I was a scoring threat. So, on and off the court I was important. When tryouts came, not too much mattered other than shooting. We had to have our vertical jump measured. I struggled to reach the lowest mark on the tape so that mine could even be recorded. In the shooting drills I was awesome, so I made the first and second cuts. The eighth graders who were trying out, including my big, strong, athletic, younger brother Frankie, were excited for me. I was the underdog, the scrappy little kid with more guts than gumption. But during the skirmishes to determine the final cut, guys guarded me like glue. I was impressively unnoteworthy on the court, and I got cut.

"This time, the feedback hurt. It said, You try hard, but you're too small. Because the coach liked me, he asked me if I wanted to be the team's equipment manager. I was devastated. I would have sooner poured hot tar in my nostrils. Again, how others treated me determined my self-esteem, and how others saw me determined how I saw myself. So what I saw was a little kid who tried hard but wasn't good enough. And, at that point, not being good enough overwhelmed me.

"Again, the feedback applied well beyond its context. My experience with basketball reflected on me as a whole—who I was and the kind of person I was. My problems under a ten-foot basket were merely symptoms of a much grander problem—that was just one of many places where a mirror could reflect what I was worth. I'm not suggesting my response was justified, but that's the way it was.

"Having found praise too difficult to come by in athletics, I began to try other things as a means for gaining recognition. I became involved in speech and drama. I did very well. I won awards at speech contests and some very pretty girls on the speech team (Debbie, in particular) wanted to be my partner for duo acting. My self-esteem rose with enthusiasm over my newfound talent. What's more, while interacting with the pretty girls on the team, I discovered that I had what others considered to be a clever sense of humor, which made people like me more. I put great effort into cultivating my humor because of the wonderful facility it gave me in interacting with girls who generally only the quarterback on the football team interacted with. My confidence and my image of myself soared with the delightful feedback I was getting from the speech and drama coaches, Debbie, and some other students who generally recognized me as someone who was really good in something. But for me, being recognized as good in something meant much more. It meant I was good.

"Before the speech and drama spotlight faded, I found a sport where being small was almost helpful. I started playing racquetball when I was fourteen. I played and practiced a lot with someone a year older, Bill, who hit the ball a little harder and was a notch better than I was. After several months, I won a tournament in my age division. Shortly thereafter, the club pro offered to give me lessons free because he saw good potential in my game. For me, that was the grand buffet of self-esteem cuisine. Racquetball eventually became the focal point of my life through the years between sixteen and nineteen. I became very good, earning a sports company equipment sponsorship and a tournament travel account from the racquetball franchise I worked for as an assistant club pro teaching lessons and running racquetball leagues. Patrons at the club watched when Frankie and I played. Real racquetball enthusiasts called the club to see when we would be playing. I competed well in state and regional tournaments, and people seemed to give me endless attention for it. Looking back, I realize I had become a selfish, egocentric, self-indulgent teenager, but at the time I got approval from people I interacted with outside of home, and I trusted their feedback implicitly in evaluating myself.

"I was a real slacker my first year of college. Any time devoted to academics detracted from my newfound wellspring of self-esteem in racquetball. At the racquetball club, there were spotlights, approval, and praise. At school, there were dim libraries and anonymity. Ooohs and ahhs from a racquetball gallery were a strong preference to a B on a grade slip that only a few people saw or cared about. The attention, approval, and reassurance of self-worth I got from a racquetball gallery was too strong, immediate, and vocal to be sacrificed for decent grades.

"Religion's influence in my life through the beginning of college was virtually insignificant. The principles taught and exemplified by my parents are the ones that really affected me. Church, generally speaking, was too much form and not enough substance to affect me very much. I subscribed to the values and morals taught in church wholly in the abstract and, predominantly, in practice. That didn't mean that the Church was true; the principles I subscribed to were a major part of virtually every Christian religion. Behaviorally, I appeared active in the Church to the uninformed observer. Intellectually,

I felt the Church was irrelevant. In my view, the Church appeared to be a repository of hypocrisy. One incident, though essentially innocent, may clarify why.

"Our priests quorum adviser taught a good lesson on keeping the Sabbath Day holy. I was impressed by the discussion of principle as a means of governing behavior. I was excited and encouraged at the principled nature of the lesson's content and impressed with the apparent conviction with which it was taught. After the lesson, the priests quorum adviser took one of the priests with him across the street to a convenience store to buy bread for the sacrament.

"I saw enough evidence similar to that to conclude that the things Mormons professed to believe on Sunday were without consequence during the week. Words came too easy. Too many members were not what they appeared to be. I saw virtue in the Church's teachings, but had no interest in participating in feigned adherence to its doctrines. Church seemed like a place where people learned to pretend they were different and unique when, in fact, they were indistinguishable from the community at large.

"And so my interest in the Church waned. That my parents faithfully attended church meetings was no longer a compelling enough reason for me to go. So I stayed away. In spite of attempts by quorum leaders and Sunday School teachers to reactivate me, I remained aloof and uncaring. My parents by no means remained neutral toward my decision. Their obvious preference was for me to attend church with them, but they chose not to press the issue in the usual way. I say 'usual way' because I was fortunate in having parents who understood that the promises of the gospel needed to be tested in their own lives as well as in the lives of their children. They considered that my testing time. But in order for me to test the validity of the gospel, I had to make some sort of an effort. My parents wouldn't just let me stay home from church without developing my spiritual self in some fashion. That is where 'unusual' really came into play.

"My father told me he was willing to accept my right to refuse participation in a church that I considered hypocritical and superficial provided I would not write the gospel off in the same manner. The gospel I would have to search out, ponder in my heart, and then pray about to validate or invalidate its veracity. And Dad would help. Because I refused to go to church, for the next year and a half Dad fixed me breakfast every Sunday morning. While we ate, we talked about spiritual matters, discussed the passages of scripture he had assigned me to read the week before, and I asked questions. Lots and lots of questions. There were times we argued. There were times we cried. And in spite of my young age, there were nights I lay on my bed and anguished.

"It would have been so much easier just to comply, to accept and be accepted. But I just couldn't figure out how sacrificing my integrity could make me a Christian.

"So we ate breakfast, talked, and studied. And in the face of my dad's most convincing arguments and my most intense prayers, I still felt nothing. I later discovered, when my spiritual awakening did come, that those Sunday morning talks provided a foundation of inquiry and learning that would serve me throughout my life."

Commentary

Up to this point, James's life was dominated by undesirable and unwelcomed external influences. Being short is no crime, but James was held hostage by it nevertheless. People who made fun of him probably didn't mean to hurt his feelings, but they did nevertheless. Most of them were probably struggling with their own need for recognition and acceptance, and making jokes about others is often part of that process. James didn't want to be self-conscious and need recognition, but he was and he did!

The result was a tragic loss of self-direction. The praise of others shaped important choices that really should come from the internal/eternal identity. Innocent and occasionally thoughtless comments by others can be devastating. Euphoria or despair hang on these comments, even though the comments may be thoughtless and meaningless. And only individuals with the emotional and spiritual strength to see the emptiness of such idle remarks can dismiss them with the healthy indifference they deserve.

From External to Internal Self-Direction

"My own spirituality was unexpectedly and rather abruptly awakened when I received my patriarchal blessing three months before my nineteenth birthday. Frankly, however, the blessing would have never taken place if it had been left entirely up to me. After a year and a half of meetings, discussions, prayers, and reading with no spiritual gains, I had about given up. I certainly had no interest in participating in a spiritual ordinance about which I had critical feelings. But both of my parents had been moved or impressed that I should receive my patriarchal blessing.

"So we talked some more, and those conversations were different—particularly with my dad. I explained my reservations and he understood them. But they didn't seem to matter. I said I wasn't worthy of a blessing, and he simply said, 'Get ready.' I said I really didn't want to, and he said that I really didn't want to disregard his parental advice on this particular topic at this particular time. Whenever my father spoke this way, I knew two things. First, he and Mom had talked—carefully! Second, when he did speak to me that way he always had good reason, and that usually meant he knew something I didn't know. So I agreed to prepare myself for the blessing as best I could, not because I wanted a blessing, but because my parents' views were not to be taken lightly at times like that.

"Religion, which had always existed only on an exterior shelf, was suddenly discovered in the core of my self. As the patriarch spoke to me, my heart was penetrated for the first time with power and spiritual warmth. What I experienced was both an internal awakening and an intellectual realization. When the blessing was over, I knew with all my heart and spirit something that I could not know with my mind. I knew that Christ lived. I knew that He had atoned for my sins. And I knew that I was expected to live up to my newfound knowledge. The principles of the gospel had come off the Sunday School chalkboard where they could be erased at the end of each lesson and had been indelibly etched in my heart where no eraser could reach. I knew it, and I knew I was accountable for what I did with it. I had experienced myself.

"At first, I was miserable. Not because I had lived a life of sin for which I needed to repent, although there was repenting to do, but because I felt an enormous weight of knowledge that I didn't care to have at the time. I now knew that I must change the way I lived, acted, talked, thought, and I frankly didn't want to. But I knew that I could not escape the feelings I had had during my patriarchal blessing. I knew everything was on the line.

"After my blessing, a value orientation emerged, which I would measure myself against. Regardless of what feedback I got from others, I now had personal expectations to meet a standard of behavior and thought that only I would know if I was true to it or not. All the praise from every racquetball fan in the world could no longer replace the self-esteem I would lose if I ignored the direction I had received. The praise could be enjoyed, but it was no longer the source of self-esteem. I now measured myself by my own conformity to what I knew

I needed to do. I needed to confront my sins. I needed to repent of my sins. And I needed to pay attention to the teachings of Christ and try to live by them. Because I knew I needed to do that, no amount of positive feedback from any external source could substitute for my failure to take those steps. To the extent that popular behavior required deviation from the standard of goodness and righteousness now within my heart, I suffered. While I could enjoy the praise, the lack of conformity to my heart's directives was becoming intolerable.

"Initially, my conversion did not require observable changes in behavior. What did change was the motivation for virtually all of my behavior. Whereas the object of my behavior had been to earn the praise of peers, the object now became to be true to the values and principles that now regulated my behavior. My approval required nothing less, and there were no substitutes for my approval and its influence on me and my behavior.

"My mission served to intensify the clarity of the principles and values I knew I was required to live by. It also lowered my tolerance for lack of conformity to my own standards. Before my mission, I expected to make a good faith effort, an honest attempt to do what was right, but I was more forgiving of my momentary lapses in orientation and behavior. Before my mission, the focus of my efforts was simply to ensure that I did not deny the knowledge I had acquired by grossly deviating from it behaviorally. With the start of my mission, and the added clarity of principles that that generated, my concern changed from avoiding denials and gross deviations to actively becoming the kind of person that adhering to gospel principles would make me. The sole measure of my self-esteem was becoming the degree to which I approved of myself. The degree to which I approved of myself hinged on the degree to which I conformed to the knowledge and principles God had shown me. My self-esteem had become completely internalized, and no one besides me had access to the internal controls. Only I knew how well I conformed, and when I conformed well, my self-esteem was high. When I conformed poorly, my self-esteem was low. But I had a measuring stick! An example will illustrate.

"In the mission field, I worked very hard. I put my heart into my mission like nothing I had ever done. Because of that, I knew the Lord was pleased with my efforts. I knew that to a large extent my behavior was congruent with my spiritual knowledge. Only a few months before my mission was to end, I was invited to a meeting with the mission president and a visiting Church leader. They talked at length about the status of the mission. They discussed the problems and challenges as well as the reasons for the mission's relatively low number of convert baptisms. They considered many possibilities, among which was the possible lack of the faithfulness and zeal of the missionaries themselves. Were they obedient and faithful enough? Were they committed to the work and showing it?

"These were compelling questions that I couldn't help but consider silently as they spoke. Our mission was one of the most difficult in the world in terms of convert baptisms. But was that sufficient reason not to have more? Could we have more baptisms if we were more faithful and worked harder? I searched my heart for answers. I ran a mental checklist of the hours I labored and of the effort I was applying in my missionary service. I believed within the deepest part of my soul that my offering to the Lord was acceptable. And as I came to my own conclusion about the question at hand, so did they.

"Our answers were not the same!

"If my self-esteem and my spirituality had still been externally regulated, I would have been totally devastated. I had no way of knowing how their conclusion might apply to the mission as a whole, but I knew I was not personally concerned. I knew I loved the Lord, I knew I had prayed for the salvation of the people I labored for, and I knew I had done all in my power to have that prayer answered.

"After my mission, the source of my self-esteem met a new, additional, nonspiritual test. I had to make up for an impressively average academic performance before my mission in order to achieve my academic goals. In that setting, my self-esteem would be governed by conformity to what I knew I expected of myself and knowing in my heart that my expectations had the Lord's approval. I expected of myself to give the very best effort I had, and whatever results obtained from those efforts had to be accepted, whether they were sufficient to attain my academic goals or not.

"I wanted to go to law school, which meant I needed two years of stellar performance. In the first battery of tests I took after my first semester back, I got mostly C's. I was surprised because I had studied so hard. Nevertheless, my self-esteem was safe because I knew I had put forth my best effort. What more could I have done? From that point on, I knew that the only threat to my self-esteem would be to let up and stop trying. Grades couldn't destroy my self-esteem, but I could destroy my self-esteem by failing to live up to my own expectations about my effort. The grades eventually came around, much better than I could ever have imagined, but my self-esteem thrived, not because of the grades, but because of the way I lived and organized my life.

"Early in my study I remembered reading the scripture, 'Seek ye first the kingdom of God and his righteousness, and all these things shall be added unto you' (3 Nephi 13:33). One of my expectations, and thus one determinant of my self-esteem, was my conformity to this principle. Had I studied on Sunday, had I compromised my academic integrity by any dishonesty, my self-esteem would have plummeted without regard to academic results. What mattered most was putting the Lord first. What mattered next was trying hard, and that's all that mattered.

"Now, with my wife and family, the same principles apply with great force. My self-esteem continues to hinge on my conforming to the knowledge I have of gospel principles. Lethargy in following those principles comes not only at the expense of my self-esteem but at the expense of the critical relationships that are the core of my life's happiness. I love my wife most when I love the Lord first. When I fail to love the Lord first and keep His commandments, everything else that matters begins to degenerate. Self-esteem is generated and maintained by conformity to the gospel without regard to the appreciation or recognition received for that conformity—which society does not appreciate anyway."

Commentary

We can see the power of Christ in awakening the internal/eternal self to the possibilities of righteous self-government. And when that happens, a process of self-development begins that can gradually but continually enhance our understanding of spiritual influences and our receptivity to them. That development occurs as follows:

1. We have the capacity to recognize and respond to spiritual influences.

2. Spiritual influences change the heart, and a changed heart affects internal attitudes and outward behavior. That internal spiritual substance gives outward religious behavior its transcendent spiritual meaning.

3. Internal spiritual substance allows us to be internally controlled and apppropriately self-directing in the righteous government of our own lives.

4. As we learn to govern our lives in a way that is congruent with the truths the internal/eternal self has already received,

we become a better receptor for additional spiritual truth and influence.

5. The pattern of spiritual development is cyclical, and when it is sustained, it leads our hearts, minds, and behavior in the direction of enduring and authentic spirituality.

The process is a cycle of knowing truth, acknowledging it, having a change of heart, and then acting upon it. In so doing, we can become like the people of King Benjamin, who were "willing to enter into a covenant with our God to do his will, and to be obedient to his commandments in all things that he shall command us, all the remainder of our days. . . . And now, because of the covenant which ye have made ye shall be called the children of Christ, his sons, and his daughters; for behold, this day he hath spiritually begotten you; for ye say that your hearts are changed through faith on his name. . . . There is no other name given whereby salvation cometh; therefore, I would that ye should take upon you the name of Christ, all you that have entered into the covenant with God that ye shall be obedient unto the end of your lives" (Mosiah 5:6–8).

Index

Absence of self-esteem, 34–35
Acceptance, need for, 134
Achievements, 86
Activity, church, 146; and
  spiritual hypocrisy, 8
Adam and Eve, 90–92
Adams, John Quincy, 32–33
Alma, on faith, 27–28
Appearances, importance of, 3,
  6–7
Approval, need for, 134
Assumptions about the social
  environment, 37–40
Avoidance, 36, 37;
  psychological, 50, 90; root of,
  61–62; forms of, 63–64;
  spiritual dimension of, 91;
  Impression Management
  style of, 93; styles of, 93, 94,
  96, 98; coping alternatives to
  styles of, 93, 95, 97, 99; Help
  Me Find the Way style of, 94;
  Walt Disney productions
  style of, 96–97; It's Written in
  the Rule Book style of, 98–

99; more techniques of, 99–
  104; fear-motivated, 105–6

Behavior, reasons behind, 6,
  128; Christian, 6
Benson, Ezra Taft, 130
Berne, Eric, 100
Broken heart and contrite
  spirit, 8, 122–23
"Bucket of love" myth, 83–84

Change of heart, 123
Character, 22
Charity: Paul's sermon on, 7–8;
  and pride, 65
Christ, power of, 151
Christlike qualities, 131
Church activity: and spiritual
  hypocrisy, 8; and self-worth,
  84
Compliance: external, 7;
  unhealthy, 87
Confidence, 41
Conflict, denying, 97
Conformity, 135

Contrite spirit and broken heart, 8
Control, need for, 98–99
Conversion, 148
Coping, 35–36, 37, 138; and behavior patterns, 50; and self-approval, 51–52; process of, 54–58; results of, 66; as a self-affirming experience, 81; with conflict, 88; as alternative to styles of avoidance, 93, 95, 97, 99; responses, 104–5; with threatening situations, 106–11
Country club crowd, 86
Criticism, 38

Denial, 61, 97
Developmental processes for spirituality and self-esteem, 53
Distortion, 61
Distress, and self-esteem, 32

Eliot, T. S., 85
Emotional well-being and self-esteem, 9
Escape, 84
Explicit tests, 108
Eternal identity, 12; and behavior, 15; Joseph Fielding Smith on, 16. See also Internal/eternal identity
Eternal nature, 120
External appearances, 19
External behavior, 20–21
External feedback, 40
External social influences, 18

Faith: in spiritual guidance, 18; development of, 27–28

Fear, 61; facing, 97–98; of failure, incapacitating, 109
Fear-motivated avoidance, 105
Feedback: negative, 38–39; external, 40
Following the leader, 87

Gospel teachings, 114
Growth, process of, 69
Groups, and needs, 38

Habits, changing, 137
Heart, change of, 114–15
Heart, the, and spiritual nature, 24
Help Me Find the Way routine, 93–94
High self-esteem, 10
Holy Ghost, promptings of the, 24
Honesty, personal, 54–55, 58, 67
Humility: and the origins of spirituality, 27; and spiritual growth, 28–29; rewards for, 29; as an internal event, 30; and self-approval, 61–62; Spencer W. Kimball on, 58; results of, 66; personal, 67, 121
Hypocrisy, David O. McKay on, 8

If It Weren't for You syndrome, 100–101
Illusions, 4
Imitation, dangers of, 18–19; allure of, 20
Impression management, 39, 86–87, 92
Inability to make decisions, 103

Inadequacy, feelings of, 62
Influences and incentives, social, 18
Insight, 54, 57
Integrity, 67
Intelligence, 16
Internal/eternal identity, 15, 18, 19, 45, 48, 120; manifestations of our, 51–52, 66; and becoming perfected, 77; power of, 132; perfecting the, 137
Internal authenticity, 19
Internal nature of self-esteem, 11
Internal quality of spirituality, 5–9
Internal risk, 88–89
Internal well-being, 51
Interpersonal risk, 89
Introspection, 54, 57
It's Written in the Rule Book style of avoidance, 98–99

Jensen, Marlin K., 128–29

Kimball, Spencer W.: on humility, 58; on teaching, 130
King Benjamin's people, conversion of, 114–15, 123

Latter-day Saint point of view, 12
Lee, Harold B., on self-respect, 9
Lewis, C. Lewis, 124
Light of Christ, 120, 121
Love, understanding the Savior's, 59–60
Low self-esteem, 1, 9–10

Madison Avenue mentality, 3
Madsen, Truman G., 25–27
Materialism, 113–14
Maxwell, Neal A.: on truth, 115–16; on superficiality, 127
McKay, David O., on hypocrisy, 8
Mediocrity, 106–7
Metaphors, temporal, 50–51
Mission, and principles and values, 148
Moroni, on charity, 7–8
Motives for spiritual growth, 6, 9
Myths about self-esteem, 82–88

Natural man, 67, 112–13
Nephi, on charity, 7

Oaks, Dallin H., on the heart, 22–24
Obedience, unquestioning, 87
Origins of self-esteem, 33–34
Overcoming selfishness, 9

Parable of external influences, 45–48
Paradox of self-esteem, 32
Patriarchal blessing and spirituality, 146–48
Personal honesty, 58
Personal integrity, 131
Personal repentance, 92
Personal security, 77
Popularity and self-esteem, 86
Praying, 121
Pre-existence, 15–16
Premortal existence, 15–16
Pride: essence of, 28–29, 64; precipitated by fear, 129–30; personal, 139–40

Priesthood ordinances, 121
Principles, applying, 79
Process of coping, 54–55
Process of growth, 69, 131, 152
Productivity and self-esteem, 85–86
Psychological avoidance, 50, 90
Psychological coping, 54–55, 67, 110–11
Psychological risk, 35–36; 88–89
Psychological well-being and self-esteem, 9

Rational man, age of the, 17–18
Rationalization, 61, 63, 71
Reality testing, 54, 57
Rejection, threat of, 39
Repentance, personal, 92
Response styles, 80
Responsibility, 41, 89–90
Retreating, 81
Risk-taking, 41, 88

Sacrament, the, 126–27
Sanctification, 69
Satan, and avoidant behavior, 91
Satir, Virginia, 100
Savior: as exemplar of process, 85; commitment to, 124
Savior's love, understanding the, 59–60
Scripture reading, 26, 121
Scriptures, the, as the word of the Lord, 116
Schlemiel and Schmaltz syndrome, 101
Secular events and spirituality, 25
Secular rituals, 25
Security, personal, 66–67

See What You Made Me Do syndrome, 102–4
Self-affirmations, 1–2
Self-aggrandizement, 28–29, 65
Self-approval, 39–40, 51–52, 94
Self-concept, 11–12
Self-contempt, 40
Self-defeating behavior, 2, 64, 78, 139
Self-directedness, 87
Self-esteem: low, 1, 9–10, 80, 134, 136; enduring personal, 5; high, 10. 34, 80; and spiritual behavior, 21–22; importance of, 32; origin of, 33–34; absence of, 34–35; definition of, 50; developing, 137
Self-esteem, model of, 10–11
Self-evaluation, 35, 36–37, 40; as a psychological reality, 39; test, 41–45; constructing, 79–81; feelings, 93
Self-government, righteous, 151–52
Self-honesty, 52
Self-image, 111
Self-importance, 78
Self-perception, 90
Self-sufficiency, 29–30
Self-talk, 1–2
Self-thoughts, negative, 1
Self-worth, 86–87
Selfishness, overcoming, 9
Separation from the Father, 83
Sexual sin, 117–18
Shortcomings, 68–69; facing up to, 73
Sins, and spiritual development, 112
Smith, Joseph Fielding, on eternal identity, 16

Social acceptance, 86
Social environment: and high self-esteem, 34; assumptions about the, 37–40
Socialization processes, 18–19
Spirit, creation of, 16
Spiritual behavior, as an expression of self-esteem, 21–22
Spiritual emptiness, 129
Spiritual guidance, capacity for, 18
Spiritual hypocrisy, and church activity, 8
Spirituality: authentic, 5–9, 22, 30–31, 152; what it is not, 24; what it is, 24–25; secular events and, 25; origins of, 27–30; con- sequences of, 30–31; meaning of, 49; cultivating, 112; heightened, 122; as a race, 131
Stress, levels of, and self-esteem, 40
Struggling, successful, 13–14
Success and self-esteem, 84
Successful living, 4–5
Superficiality, 127

Teachable, being, 67
Technological sophistication, 17–18

Temporal metaphors, 50–51
Testimonies, and spirituality, 25
Trivializing, 125–29, 131
Truth: definition of, 115–16; perceptions of, 117–18; counter-feit, 119; receptor of, 120–22; of things of the Spirit, 125

Unconditional love, myth of,82–83
Understanding the Savior's love, 59–60

Verbal pretense, 2
Violence in marriage, 69–77

Walt Disney Productions style of avoidance, 96–98
Well-being, psychological, and self-esteem, 9
Widtsoe, John A., on testimony, 119
Will of God, implementing, 113
Winning and self-esteem, 84
Word of the Lord, scriptures as, 116
Worthlessness, feelings of, 66

"Yes" monster, 55–57
"Yes" syndrome, 55–58
Young, Brigham, on personal growth, 69